EBURY
PA

Shweta Singh Kirti, a fashion designer trained at India's National Institute of Fashion Technology (NIFT), transformed her career trajectory after obtaining an MBA in the USA. Her fusion of business acumen and spirituality birthed into a passion project called Damara Kids, an online mindfulness programme for children. Here, she imparts mindfulness and meditation techniques, fostering focus, concentration and self-mastery, empowering them to unleash their potential.

Beyond her role with Damara Kids, Shweta is deeply involved in several non-profit initiatives and has served on the board of OMniAwareness. As a public figure with a substantial following, she serves as an inspiration to many, standing as a thought leader in the realms of holistic well-being and spiritual enlightenment. Following the tragic loss of her brother, Sushant Singh Rajput, she embarked on several months of extensive solitary retreats. This profound and transformative experience gave birth to her first book, *Pain: A Portal to Enlightenment*.

Celebrating 35 Years of
Penguin Random House India

ADVANCE PRAISE FOR THE BOOK

'A profound and heartfelt exploration of the human experience, *Pain: A Portal to Enlightenment* beautifully navigates the journey from suffering to spiritual awakening'—Kangana Ranaut, actor

'In the Buddhist tradition, it is said that pain is inevitable, but suffering is optional. In her brilliant new book, Shweta Singh Kirti explores how we can move through grief to become stronger and more spiritually attuned. We can't escape loss in this lifetime, yet Shweta shows readers how we can transform ourselves through the pain and grow from the experience'—Lissa Coffey, bestselling author of *Closure and the Law of Relationship: Endings as New Beginnings* and co-creator of *Song Divine: The Bhagavad Gita Rock Opera*

'Prepare to be spellbound by this extraordinary literary gem! It is magic on paper, alchemizing the profound depths of human suffering into a phoenix-like rise from the ashes after the losing a loved one'—Ajay Bhutoria, author, entrepreneur, political strategist and community leader

'A sincere seeker's awe-inspiring real-life story of healing, self-discovery and transformation. Guaranteed to give enormous strength, spiritual wisdom and coping tools to anyone dealing with trauma of losing loved ones. Blessings!'—Sejal Shah, yoga teacher trainer and author of four ebooks on yoga

'This is one of the best books I have read till date—deep, simple and profound'—Radhakrishnan Pillai, bestselling author and founder of Atma Darshan and Chanakya Aanvikshiki

'A compelling narrative on navigating life's most intricate yet unavoidable emotion'—Kushal M. Choksi, bestselling author of *On a Wing and a Prayer*

PAIN

A Portal to Enlightenment

Shweta Singh Kirti

EBURY
PRESS

An imprint of Penguin Random House

EBURY PRESS

USA | Canada | UK | Ireland | Australia
New Zealand | India | South Africa | China | Singapore

Ebury Press is part of the Penguin Random House group of companies
whose addresses can be found at global.penguinrandomhouse.com

Published by Penguin Random House India Pvt. Ltd
4th Floor, Capital Tower 1, MG Road,
Gurugram 122 002, Haryana, India

First published in Ebury Press by Penguin Random House India 2023

ISBN 9780143461364

Typeset in Adobe Caslon Pro by Manipal Technologies Limited, Manipal

www.penguin.co.in

This work is lovingly dedicated to the memory of my dear brother, Sushant Singh Rajput. His brilliance, passion and boundless creativity continue to inspire me every day. Through this book, I aim to honour his legacy and share the light he brought into the world.

Endowed with the blessings of Gurudev Sri Sri Ravi Shankar for the profound wisdom in this book and carries forth his heartfelt wishes for its success

Prayer

May all be ever happy and ever peaceful

Contents

Foreword

Swami Sarvapriyananda

All our lives, we strive to overcome suffering and attain fulfilment. Transcending suffering and attaining deep, lasting happiness has been the goal of the Indian spiritual–philosophical traditions (*darsanas*). The darsanas——such as Vedanta, Yoga, Tantra, etc.—have an optimistic view, that it is indeed possible to attain freedom from suffering.

The vast variety of practices found in the darsanas have been broadly classified into four yogas by Swami Vivekananda: Karma (action), Bhakti (devotion), Raja (meditation) and Jnana (knowledge). Our suffering is often exacerbated by our endless obsession with our little selves. Instead of endlessly focusing on our minute personal feelings, complaints and demands, Karma Yoga teaches us to be bigger, to be selfless.

Selflessness, rather counter-intuitively, actually pays more than selfishness, but it requires maturity to understand this. Bhakti is the most powerful support in trying circumstances. All our desires are given up in one great love for God. We are no longer alone, but we have the mighty support of the Divine in our lives. Raja Yoga, the way of meditation, gives us the power of focus. What we focus upon and how much we focus determine the quality of our lives. By focusing on the positive, on the constructive and on the Divine (instead of the mundane), the quality of our inner lives improves dramatically. Finally, self-knowledge, as cultivated in Jnana Yoga, shows us the deepest dimension of our being, which is ever untouched by sorrow. 'Having attained which nothing greater remains to be got, being centred in which, the heaviest of sorrows cannot move one' (Bhagavad Gita 6.22).

Selflessness, devotion, focus and self-knowledge help us transcend pain. Our response to situations which would be ordinarily seen as painful, changes dramatically. We can be peaceful and composed even amidst challenging circumstances.

In the world that we live in, the insights of modern neuroscience and medicine cannot be, and should not be, ignored. The author has carefully researched the literature on the science of pain and relief from pain. The results of that extensive study are also presented in these pages.

Do these methods actually work? The importance of this volume lies in its testimony to the fact that spirituality is indeed the deep solution to suffering. The author, in the face of trauma and deep personal pain, made a determined and systematic effort to overcome suffering through spiritual practice. Her primary paths are bhakti, Advaitic self-inquiry, and the Tibetan Buddhist knowledge and meditation practices. She records her practices, breakthroughs and results meticulously in the pages that follow.

Ultimately, it is up to the individual seeker. Pain is a wake-up call. How much longer will you suffer? Awaken out of the slumber of complacency, arise to your real spiritual nature and stop not till the goal is reached.

May this volume be a blessing to millions around the world trying to transcend suffering and find fulfilment.

Introduction

The Origin and Purpose of This Book

Everyone understands pain and suffering; it is something that we all share. It is utterly intimate yet universally shared.

Buddha said, 'The world is filled with pain and sorrow. But I have found a serenity, which you can find too.'

And indeed, we can find the serenity the Buddha is talking about. Pain itself can become our portal to enlightenment. When everything is going well, despite the undercurrents of dissatisfaction, we don't tend to move towards spirituality. However, when our world is turned upside down by a tumultuous event, there is no other option but to gather the pieces of our upended life with the timeless wisdom of faith and spirituality. The worst kind of loss one can suffer may be in what it takes to become a Buddha.

Death is the greatest pain and a fact of life, yet we fail to notice it until our own loved one dies. *What is death? Will I die too?* This is our inherent subconscious fear, but one that we are rarely aware of. All human beings are born with this existential angst and until and unless we find an answer to the universal questions of death and suffering, we can't find any peace.

Life has a way of imparting its lessons through painful experiences that we just cannot avoid. It is through these moments that we come to realize we have been constructing sandcastles without any solid foundation. We chase after money, fame, relationships and dreams, only to find that the fulfilment of one dream leads to the emergence of many others, leaving us perpetually unsatisfied. This book is an invitation to ground ourselves so deeply in our true essence that even if the waves of life come and wash away our sandcastles, we remain unshaken. It is a transformative journey that requires us to let go of our illusions and awaken to the truth within. Let this book take you by the hand and lead you to a place of authentic Beingness, where you can find the inner peace and fulfilment that you have been searching for.

Buddha said that life is suffering, and I never understood this until I lost my mom. Losing her shifted the very grounds of my existence. I had barely been able to pull myself out of the grief when the inevitable got replayed in my life again, and that too with an unimaginable intensity. My younger brother, the late Bollywood actor Sushant Singh Rajput, was found dead in his Mumbai apartment in mysterious circumstances. Prima facie, the death looked like suicide. His passing took the world by storm, especially the 1.8 billion people with roots in the Indian subcontinent. I started getting calls and messages from countless people who claimed they wanted to kill themselves as well and that if Sushant Singh Rajput, a big film star, could not deal with his problems, their hopelessness was justified, or so they rationalized. All this was a heavy weight on my shoulders. Not only did I have to deal with my own grief, but I also had to alleviate the pain felt by thousands of others who reported falling into depression after hearing the news. I was thrust into the public domain with immense responsibility. While I was able to calm some people down and reported their intentions to their family members and authorities whenever I could, we did lose some of Sushant's fans to suicide. It was a dark and despairing time. I had always thought of myself as a strong person until I was forced to collect the debris from the storm that had hit my life.

I have healed and transformed a lot since then. My pain and grief have fuelled my transformation journey and in this first book of mine, I would like to share the techniques and processes I utilized to transform pain into eternal, unshakable peace. It is my ardent desire that this book inspires you to live a life of meaning and purpose in the aftermath of losing a loved one.

I prefer not to identify with my storyline. But the conviction of sharing my story for the benefit of others was strengthened when, during a solitary retreat, I came across a chapter titled 'Universal Responsibility' in a Buddhist text. I knew then that something greater wanted to express itself through me and my story. I had gone to the solitary retreat during this phase of upheaval in my life with two things in my mind and heart—the deep pain of losing my only brother in a

tragic way and the belief I had in the concept of non-duality.*
As I spent those months in meditation and contemplation, I
integrated the knowledge of non-duality, realizing that my
true nature is nothing but the universal consciousness, and
that enabled the transformation of my pain into something
beautiful.

This is what I seek to convey through the medium of this
book, to help you awaken to your true nature and transcend all
kinds of suffering. Pain and suffering are two different things;
'pain is inevitable, but suffering is optional'. Resistance to pain
leads to suffering. Pain can be used as one of the portals to
enlightenment.

Enlightenment is not a dead or elusive state that can
only be realized sometime in the future or somewhere in
an ideal space. It is in every moment if only we choose it.
Most of us go about life focusing on our personal stories
and seldom do we realize that personal stories can limit us
in many ways, making us feel separate from other beings,
weighing us down. Our stories make us cling to our egos
and that further solidifies our existence as separate from the
universal consciousness. We need to let go of the burden
of our personal stories and melt into the embrace of the
infinite to realize ourselves as that One Eternal Spirit. After
which, only love can flow from and through us. It leaves no
space for any division—me and mine, you and yours, they
and them—the meaning that these separators hold ceases to
exist altogether.

---

* Non-duality claims that there is a single universal consciousness (One
Eternal Spirit) and everything in the universe is an inseparable part of it.

Humans have an innate need to connect with fellow humans. This is the cosmic design and if we do not come together in peace and harmony, drunk with the divinity of our souls, there is no transcendence for us. A growing number of us are awakening to our true calling, recognizing the essence of our being. But as long as we remain fixated on the personal narratives within our minds, we cannot experience the eternal joy that awaits us. We must hold each other's hands and form a circle of unity and light the fire of knowledge in which we throw away all the personal mental garbage that holds us back. The song we will sing then will have the melody of eternity, and the dance we will do then will have the rhythm of infinity. Our rejoicing together will then defy and surpass every narrative of love and ecstasy. This is the vision of a pure land, the heaven on earth. Let us all come together to consciously create this reality.

* * *

You may ask why I think I can take you on this journey of transformation. My answer to this would be that I have put many hours into my spiritual practice and have also had my fair share of breakthrough experiences. I have suffered from several blows of trauma and have channelled all the pain into my spiritual life that has bloomed into a beautiful, bittersweet, ongoing journey of personal transformation.

Before I dive in, I would like to elaborate a little on the organization of this book. I begin by talking about my background and story in this introductory chapter, as well as my breakthrough experiences. In Chapter 1, I cover the science behind pain and trauma to illustrate how trauma affects various aspects of our lives, including physical and mental health. I also elaborate on the impact of childhood trauma, because research on pain and trauma has shown that childhood events are impactful and more likely to affect our lives adversely. The impact of grief caused by the death of loved ones is also discussed because that has been the core of my own pain. In Chapter 2, I discuss why pain leads to suffering even though suffering is optional while pain is inevitable. This chapter delves a little deeper into the spiritual concepts where it is discussed that the root cause of suffering is our mistaken belief that we are nothing more than individual bodies, minds and personalities. In Chapter 3, I discuss the techniques available to avoid suffering and how to use pain to catapult ourselves into enlightenment. In Chapter 4, I explore how we can experience life with a stable base of unshakable peace. This chapter also points out the impediments one will encounter while trying to establish such a life. Finally, in Chapter 5, I discuss the outcome if we follow the processes discussed in the previous chapters.

My aspiration in sharing my story is to serve as a compassionate, empathetic guide for my readers. It is my wish that by sharing my personal journey and spiritual experiences, I can offer assistance to those seeking to transform their own pain into a foundation for an awakened, holistic life.

Let us commence this journey, and I look forward to meeting you on the other side.

My Story of Love and Loss

My Background

I grew up in a big family, during the simpler times of the 1980s and 1990s, in Patna, the capital city of Bihar. I belonged to a family of seven, with relatives visiting and living with us for short durations now and then. My beautiful family was led by my strong-willed mother Usha Singh and my nonchalant father Krishna Kishore Singh.

My father was a risk-taking machine, an entrepreneur of his time. He was the only one from his family to leave his ancestral wealth and venture to a big city. While Patna isn't a big city compared to Mumbai or Delhi, it is indeed cosmopolitan in contrast to my father's ancestral roots. My father did fairly well both at his job and his enterprises, at least until I graduated from high school.

My mother was the *yin* to my father's *yang*. She anchored us so that we could explore the world courageously, knowing that we had the safety and security of our mother's love at home. Words fall short when I try describing her—*Mumma*, as I called her, was such a force of nature. She laughed so hard that the sound of her laughter would easily travel a mile and people would know it was her laughter. She had the best sense of humour. On our walks, she would quietly pass such funny comments on passers-by that I would have to fight hard to not crack up in front of the stranger, while my belly wanted to blow up in smithereens with laughter.

Her beauty was unmatched; her features were chiselled. God used the best craftsmanship while creating her. My dad saw her eyes and fell in love with her. He told everyone that he wanted to marry the girl who had '*hirni jaisi aankhen*' (doe eyes).

As a mother, she was the most loving, the best mentor and motivator. She brought us up in a way that convinced us that nothing was impossible. She always told us that the sky is the limit, never feeding us any concepts of limitations. We knew we could win the world as she was the wind beneath our wings; we were all set to fly high, as she dreamt for us.

I was a very emotional child; I still am a very emotional person. It was always difficult for me to find words to express myself. This is still one of my shortcomings. Though I was never able to tell Mumma how much I loved her in words, by God's grace I was able to bring her pride and joy in my own little ways. She always called me her most beautiful child and often nibbled on my little fingernail and spat it on my face to keep the evil eye away. How sweet is that! She even called me '*gaai*', someone who is as simple as a cow, and she worried about my well-being in this difficult world. She would say, 'I have given you to God, He will take care of you.'

I remember how she would always encourage me. Once, I was sketching a portrait on a chart paper and I sat for over three hours straight working on it. She praised me to the skies, appreciating my concentration power and talent. Despite my lack of training in art, she said, my sketch was much better than those who were actually trained in it. Whenever I did something with my heart and soul, she would appreciate the hard work that I put in the job, no matter how big or small it was.

She filled me up with so much confidence that everything felt achievable. I was a good athlete in school and had made a district record by winning golds in all four track and field events I had participated in. Once when I was training for the district level, my Physical Training teacher (we called him 'PT sir') had set up the high-jump bar corresponding to the height maintained for state-level championships. I remember I kept trying to cross it but failed again and again. It had got late in the evening and I was still trying to cross the bar even then, and that's when I heard a cracking sound as I landed on the sand. I had dislocated my ankle. PT sir ran towards me, really worried. After tending to me, he told me that we should wrap up. But I refused. I had set my sights on crossing the bar. And I remember I limped to the starting point to jump one last time. I put my heart and soul into it, ran and jumped . . . and what a jump it was! I had finally crossed the bar. That day I knew for a fact that nothing was impossible. The truth of mind over matter shone forth. My mom's words were becoming a reality.

I was so attached to Mumma that when I travelled out of town, I would carry her sari with me and sleep holding it. She smelled of sandalwood, as did her clothes. She had given me Rs 500 to spend on myself, but the best thing I could think of buying for myself was the smile on her face, so I bought a handbag and a sari for her from Delhi. When I presented them to her, she tapped me on my forehead, saying in a firm voice, 'Is this what you have bought for yourself, *pagli*?' I would massage her body every evening and the day I wouldn't, my own legs would start hurting. I can't express in words how much joy it brought me to see a smile on her face. And I used my accomplishments to make her proud.

Coming of Age

I kept setting goals for myself to make my mumma happy. I planned to get into Notre Dame for my junior and senior years of high school. It was the only school I applied to, because my mother wanted her daughter to go there. So I did, cracking the entrance examination for Notre Dame and finishing high school from there. At the time of my selection, my parents were called for an interview. My dad and mom hardly spoke English and I was the one answering all the questions on their behalf. I remember the principal of the school, Sister Beena, praising me for my accomplishments in sports, education, debates and extracurricular activities. She felt that Notre Dame might not be able to offer me enough exposure in sports. I saw my parents' chests swelling with pride. At the end of the interview, as we walked out, my mom kissed me on my forehead and that was my biggest accomplishment.

Then I aimed my sights on getting into NIFT (National Institute of Fashion Technology, the premier Indian school for fashion). I worked hard and stayed focused. On the very first try, I cracked the written and creative entrance exams. We received the summons for the interview. At that time, my second sister Rubi di's marriage was being planned. Rajput weddings are big events and everyone was occupied with the preparations, so there was no one who could take me to Kolkata for the interview. I cried to God, assured that He would take care of everything. Magically, everything fell in place. Pinky di (my eldest sister Rani di's friend) called up. She lived in Kolkata and was married to an income tax officer. When my mom mentioned my NIFT interview in Kolkata, she told her not to worry about a thing and that she would take care of it all.

A chauffeur-driven car and a beautiful guest house was arranged for me. Chunnu bhaiya, a cousin, accompanied me to Kolkata. The evening before my interview, we visited the Dakshineswar Kali Temple. I still remember every bit of that visit. It was the most stunning experience of my life. As we stood in the long queue for Maa's *darshan* (auspicious sighting), I touched the outer walls of the temple. It was as if something deep had been stirred in my heart; tears started flowing down my cheeks. As any regular teenager, I felt extremely embarrassed about crying in public. But despite my embarrassment, tears kept rolling down my cheeks while I tried hard to not let any sound escape my mouth. After completing a circumambulation of the temple, we reached right in front of the powerful *murti* (idol). As I entered the inner shrine, the priest tapped something on my head. I was so completely taken by the presence of the divine that I was totally unaware of my surroundings. The drill was to go to the front and pray and leave. Nobody could stand there for long as the queues were always long. As I reached the front, I started crying profusely. I wasn't able to stop myself any more, my knees felt weak and I fell in front of the idol, asking, 'Why did you separate me from you? Where did I go wrong? Do you not feel my pain? Are you happy to see me cry? I won't leave until you answer.' And the stubborn kid that I was, I ready set to die unless I got my answers. My heart felt like it was being painfully wrenched out, draining every last drop of my tears until none were left to shed.

Then from the corner of my eye, I noticed an elderly woman making her way towards me, walking in the opposite direction of the exit. Although it appeared highly unlikely that anyone would make their way through that path given the massive crowds, she seemed to navigate through the crowd with ease, moving closer and closer towards me. Suddenly, she stumbled and reached out for support, her hand landing gently on my head. I felt a surge of energy coursing down my spine, and a sense of calm washed over me as if a cool breeze had blown through me. I looked up to see that the woman had white hair and was wearing a white sari. But before I could even process what had happened, she had vanished without a trace, leaving me bewildered and searching for answers. As I struggled to come out of the crowd, I was completely squished. I used to be very thin then. I thought to myself that it was okay if I died in God's abode. As soon as that thought crossed my mind, somebody held my hand in the crowd and almost pulled me out by force. When I emerged from the throng, I saw Chunnu bhaiya standing in front, and I asked him, '*Bhaiya, aapne nikala mujhe* [Did you pull me out]?'

He answered, '*Nahi, main to tumhara itne der se wait kar raha hoon, kahan thi tum* [No, I have been waiting for you for so long, where were you]?'

Later, I realized I had forgotten to pray for my interview as intense *Viraha* (feeling of separateness) had taken over me.

The next day, I went to NIFT Kolkata (although I was admitted to NIFT Chennai, Kolkata was my interview location). It was a beautiful building. The first task was a situational test where we were given materials to depict a celebration. I had a plan in mind to make a champagne bottle and sofas, but somehow it didn't work out. I had used all the materials given to me, but there was this small piece of silver cardboard still left. I called upon God for help. He told me not to worry. He told me to make a sweet-box with the leftover cardboard piece. I did that. Then there was a pin. He asked me to carve a beautiful design on top by making small dots on the cardboard. By the end of it, the sweet-box turned out to be exotic, something quite creative, different from what others had made. The interview went like a breeze, because before the interview, a bunch of seniors from NIFT had started hazing me in a friendly fashion. They asked me the same questions that were put to me during the interview. They refined my answers and prepared me for the session. It was God's way of getting me ready for the interview.

By the end, I knew I had done pretty well. When the result was published, my rank was 102. I was thrilled and ran to mom to inform her about my result. She was in the puja (prayer) room. It was dusk and she was performing Friday *vrat puja* (worshipping while fasting) for Lakshmi Maa (a Hindu Goddess). Full of joy, I told her about the result. She was overcome with gratitude and asked me to thank God. My mother always told me that whatever I wanted to say, I should say it to God—He always listens. And I knew that for a fact.

Mom and Dad accompanied me to Chennai and helped me settle down. Mumma was very happy to see the newly built NIFT building—it was colourful, very well designed, in short, very Nifty! The NIFT hostel was equally beautiful; the bathroom looked like that of a five-star hotel, decked with floor-to-ceiling mirrors. Mom was smitten by the beauty of the campus. She kissed me on my forehead to let me know how proud she was of me. That would turn out to be a goodbye kiss, the last kiss from her. I was close to tears, as Mom and Dad were leaving. But Dad kept his finger on his lips, gesturing for me to not cry as that would have saddened Mom as well. So, I didn't; I kept it all inside. I didn't know then that it was the last time I was seeing her alive.

It was July 2002 when I went to Chennai and by December 2002, she was no more. The foundation of my being was lost on that dark December day. My mind raced with questions. *For whom will I do anything now? Who will be proud of me? Who will kiss me on my forehead again if I do something right? Why do I have to live after losing her?* All my dreams came crashing down. I suffered a lot, and a lot of weird things started happening to me. As my mind tried to process the grief and this deep loss, I would often find myself struggling with sleep paralysis. At that time, I thought it was some kind of ghost haunting me. I had decided not to trouble

Dad with any of my needs and to learn to be self-sufficient. As Sushant bhai and Sonu di were studying in Delhi at that time, Dad already had his responsibilities and I didn't want to add to his worries. I started working for L'Oréal as their beauty consultant and did modelling gigs. I earned enough to pay for my college tuition, hostel and bills. As a matter of fact, as a token of love, I would send money to Dad every month. I was trying to make my mom proud. But the modelling/acting space felt like a very shallow, murky world to me. I found the people in those fields self-centred. One of my friends helped me a lot then. He would drive me to different shoots, care for me as family and protect me from the outside world. I will be ever thankful to him.

Family Life

Vishal (my husband) and I started dating in 2004. He was studying Electrical Engineering at IIT (Indian Institute of Technology, the elite engineering institute of India) Chennai. We knew each other from middle school. We had gone to the same middle school and also attended the first two years of high school at St Karen's together. Vishal's love healed me; he wrapped me in his warmth and showered me with the motherly affection I was craving. He became home and everything to me. I could talk to him about anything. He was always there for me and accepted me completely. We got married in 2007.

Our marriage was special too—we didn't take a penny from our parents. I had seen my father struggle through Rani di's and Rubi di's weddings. As I said, Rajput weddings are big affairs; a lot of money is spent. I wanted my father to relax and enjoy his daughter's wedding without any headaches.

Rani di and her husband, my *Jiju,* helped me with all the wedding arrangements. I remember buying dresses for my family members to wear at the wedding as I was the fashion designer of the family. It gave me much joy and filled my heart with immense satisfaction. Everything flowed wonderfully and we were married without a hitch.

Vishal was living in the US at the time. He came down to India to get married and took me to the US post our wedding. We had our first child, Freyjaa, in 2008. My life changed, and I learned how special it was to be a mother. Life in the US was difficult. I didn't have a work visa and felt like an outsider for the first few years. My self-esteem and confidence diminished as, not being free to work, I felt chained. But I utilized the time and poured myself into the spiritual quest I was so passionate about. I read books, listened to lectures and meditated day in, day out. Through a friend, I was introduced to the teachings of an enlightened Hindu sage called Ramana Maharshi. His teachings on spirituality transformed my life for good. I felt more complete than I had ever felt before. I knew I had found a *brahmastra* (weapon of the gods) to cut through the delusions. I transferred my NIFT credits and got a bachelor's degree in the US and then went on to get an MBA. Here too, I hit a roadblock as it was difficult to get an H-1B sponsorship if one were not from the tech field. I had my second child, Nirvanh, in 2015. The following year, I started Damara Kids, an after-school centre to teach kids about mindfulness, meditation and yoga. I had begun to learn to spiritualize my whole life and to practise being aware moment-to-moment.

Losing Loved Ones

I was exposed to the death of a loved one very early in my life. Those who are familiar with our family are aware that we were five sisters and two brothers, in the following sequence: My first brother, Rani di (Neetu), Rubi di (Meetu), Bobby di, Sonu di (Priyanka), me (Shweta) and Gulshan (Sushant). My parents' first child, my eldest brother, had been born at a time when infant mortality rates used to be high. He didn't survive long, but this event had happened many years before my arrival and did not impact me in a big way.

However, we lost Bobby di when I was eight years old. Bobby di was an angel. She kept her appearance very simple but her mannerisms were divine and par excellence. She would take care of Mumma's every need and shower the little ones with all the love possible. I remember her washing our feet and hands and putting moisturizer on them after we got back from school. She herself was very young then.

There is another incident that comes to my mind. While playing, I once dropped a big can of oil in the storeroom. Bobby di saw the situation and asked me to hide so she could take the blame. I clearly remember going and hiding on the terrace, but when I heard her getting scolded by Mom, I couldn't take it. My integrity awoke, at the age of seven. I went down and accepted my mistake, telling Mom that she should be scolding me, not her, as it was my fault. I got my share of scolding. Later, when Bobby di inquired why I had to do that when she had already taken a scolding on my behalf, I told her that I couldn't let her be scolded, especially for something she wasn't at fault for . . . then she hugged me and we both cried. I don't have many memories of us, but one thing I know for sure is that she was not of this world. She was an angel who went back to where she belonged.

I still remember trying to wake her up when I saw her corpse. Death was an unfamiliar concept at that age. When I saw my mom cry aloud, it shattered my heart. I shook Bobby di's body, pleading: 'Mom is crying now. Wake up, you shouldn't cause Mumma any more pain.' I thought it was some kind of a game, a play, that she would actually get up in a bit. But as people gathered in my house, an uncle picked me up in his arms and told me that didi wouldn't wake up again, 'She is with God now.' It was then that an intense, unknown pain started to grip me.

Mother's Death

I have already mentioned that I lost my mother in December 2002, when I had barely turned eighteen. As I lay on my bed one night, with the door open, I had a strange nightmare through half-open eyes. In the darkness, I saw Kali Maa, the dark Hindu Goddess, with her eyes wide open and her red tongue hanging out, walk up to me. As she came close, she reached out for my heart, her hand going deep inside my chest as if my body lay there almost porous. I clearly saw her pulling something out, and as she did, my upper body was lifted up from the bed by the sheer impact. I sat up, awake, with a feeling of loss . . . an inexplicable emptiness. I knew something had happened though the news had not reached me yet. I was studying at NIFT, Chennai, during that time and our semester finals were going on.

A teacher of mine was informed about my mother's death by Rani di. My teacher made me talk to Rani di. She told me, 'Mom is in a coma. You come back after finishing your exams and we will hold Mumma's hands, talk to her and pull her out of the coma.' After which, she broke down and cried. I played along and gave her the strength that, yes, we would get her out of the coma. While I didn't know what a coma was back then, I had this deep sense that we had lost her even though I hadn't explicitly been told as much. I submitted all my assignments for the finals and took off for Patna. A very good friend came along to be my support. Mom's death was the straw that broke the camel's back. Bobby di's passing had exposed me to the trauma of death. My mother's death broke me for a long while until I got married and started my own family. The process of healing has taken several years. While I still miss her every day, there is a calm acceptance of the event and I have centred into the peace of her everlasting love.

Brother's Death

My family members have often told me that Mom and Dad wanted a son, more so because Mumma's first child had been a son and she had lost him at a very young age. Mom and Dad were very hopeful for a second son. They took a *sankalp* (vow) and prayed to Bhagwati Maa (Hindu Goddess) for two years straight. They fasted, meditated, performed pujas, *havans* (fire rituals), and went to spiritual places and met spiritual people. But then I was born, on the day of Diwali (Indian festival of lights). Mumma considered me very lucky and often called me Lakshmi-ji (Hindu Goddess worshipped on Diwali). They continued with their *sadhna* (practice) and kept praying for a son, and a year later, my little brother was born. Right from the beginning, he was a charmer, mesmerizing everyone with his beautiful smile and twinkling eyes.

So, this little one was my '*Pithiya*'. This is a term used in colloquial Hindi to signify the one who comes right after you. Mumma believed that I was the catalyst for his much-desired arrival into our lives and I accepted the honour wholeheartedly. Being protective of him was second nature to me, as I felt a profound sense of responsibility for bringing him into this earthly plane.

Growing up, we were each other's shadows—always together. We played and danced, studied and got into mischief, ate and slept, and did everything in unison, to the point where people forgot we were two separate individuals; they even called us 'Gudia-Gulshan' as if we were a single entity (Bhai's nickname was Gulshan and mine Gudia).

When we started preschool, we had to go to different classes. Bhai's nursery (for three-year-olds) and my prep (for four-year-olds) classes were in the same building, so we managed our first year of school pretty well. But my kindergarten class was in a different building, while his prep classroom remained in the same building, so we got separated. One day, after lunch break was over, I saw Bhai in my classroom. We were just four or five years old then. Though happy, I was completely shocked to see him and asked him how he had got there—his building was at least a quarter-mile away. He told me that he was feeling alone and anxious, and wanted to be with me. How adventurous and courageous he was to escape his building, sneak out and then walk nearly half a kilometre to enter my building right under a watchman's nose and finally find my class and me. I found his explanation for running pretty valid as I knew that feeling. When I was dropped off at school for the first time, I had kept crying and asking Dad not to leave me. Now, as a five-year-old protective elder sister, I assured him that he could be with me. I tried to hide him between my friend and me, but somehow my class teacher noticed him while marking the attendance. I was a little scared, but to protect my little brother, I stood up and told her that he was not feeling well and asked if he could stay with us until dismissal. To my amazement, the teacher agreed and we were so happy. He was sent back to his building after two classes. He was so happy to sit next to me for those two classes, liberated from his angst by the time he was sent back.

In the sixth grade, I experienced another significant milestone—my first period. My mother took Gulshan aside and instructed him to be gentle with me. Otherwise, we would spend all day playfully hitting each other just like young animals do. Naturally, he was curious about why he had been given such an instruction. Mumma had explained to me how to dispose of the pad, and while I was doing that one day, he followed me to the trash can and inquired, 'What is it that you can't share with me? I don't like this barrier between us.' It was a testament to his remarkable sensitivity and our profound closeness.

Fast forward to 2007, the day of my wedding. As I prepared to leave, Bhai hugged me tightly, tears streaming down our faces. It was a heartbreaking moment—we knew that we wouldn't be living together any more, that we wouldn't have the luxury of seeing each other as often as we used to. But we made a promise to one another that we'd always be there for each other, no matter the distance. As I settled into my new life in the US, I couldn't shake the feeling of regret for leaving my brother behind. Yet, despite the miles that separated us, I made sure to always be there for him. If anyone ever spoke ill of him, I'd immediately rush to his defence. I am content that my conscience is clear, and that I never wavered in my love and support for my dear brother.

As the years went by, both of us got swept up in the hustle and bustle of life. My brother's rise to stardom in Bollywood made us all incredibly proud, but I remained fiercely protective of him. Whenever we spoke, I'd urge him to come to visit me in the US so that we could escape the noise and relive our childhood memories. Over the years, I made several trips to India to visit him while he was pursuing his acting career, visiting in 2014, 2015, 2016 and 2017. I could not visit India in 2018 and 2019 but made a trip in January 2020 especially to see him. However, due to the complicated set of circumstances he was in, I could not meet him. But when we got to talk on the phone, I showered him with a lot of love and assured him of my support.

I would rather not go into great detail about my brother's death. However, I feel it is important to note that just a few days before his passing, on 10 June, I had invited him to the US. He expressed a sincere desire to visit and spend time with me. I had planned to take him hiking, engage in some fun activities and just enjoy each other's company in California. Unfortunately, due to the Covid-19 pandemic, it was not possible for him to make the trip.

On the fateful night of 13 June, as I lay in bed, I found myself feeling uneasy and, strangely enough, began discussing the topic of death and the soul's journey with Vishal. It was only after I had convinced myself, through reason and contemplation, that the soul continues to exist even after the body's demise that I was able to finally drift off to sleep. However, in the middle of the night, Vishal's phone began ringing incessantly. After getting up to use the bathroom, he returned with the news that Bhai had taken his own life. He shouted out to me, 'Shweta, Sushant is no more!' A chill ran down my spine and I lay in bed paralysed. I didn't scream. I didn't cry. By conviction of my practice, I fell into a space that sucked all the shock that my body and mind were going through.

Finally, I gathered courage and rose from my bed to check my phone. I had several missed calls from Rani di. When I called her back, she could only weep uncontrollably, '*Guram, Gulshan nai raha. Kuch samajh main nai aa raha*' (Guram, Gulshan is no more. I don't understand what happened), she exclaimed. I tried my best to console her, but I was at a loss for words.

After Rani di broke the news of Bhai's death, I immediately called my sister, Rubi di, who was in Mumbai at the time. Over the next few days, I kept in constant touch with her. My heart went out to her as she had to see Bhai's lifeless body and deal with the police and media. I don't think I would have had the strength to cope if I were in her place. But she is the strongest among us.

I felt a sense of urgency to be there for my brother's final farewell, but due to the Covid-19 situation, regular flights to India were not operating. I had to find a way to get there. Fortunately, many people came together to help, and I was able to secure a ticket. However, while I was still in the US, Bhai's body was cremated. The realization that I would not be able to see him for the last time and bid him a proper farewell left me feeling angry and devastated. There was no closure for me. As I struggled with these emotions, I asked myself a difficult question: *If I had been there, would I have been able to watch his body burn in front of my eyes?* The answer was a resounding no. Even the thought of it was too much to bear. I remember going into my closet that day and crying loudly. The grief had already set in, and I could barely contain the pain. I just needed time to grieve and process the reality of the situation.

Upon arriving in India, the first thing I did was to embrace Rani di. Even though everything felt disorienting, I had a clear mission in mind. My goal was to make sure that my brother's final rites were conducted in a spiritually meaningful way and to give him the best send-off possible. Over the next few days, we performed the *Garuda Puran path* (readings from an ancient Hindu text), sang *bhajans*, meditated and prayed for my brother's departed soul to find peace. Bhai visited me in my dreams and we talked for hours together. I asked him a lot of questions and he answered them to my satisfaction. We hugged and kissed. When I got up the next day, I clearly remembered Bhai's touch and how it felt when we hugged;

it felt more real than the real world. But I did not remember the contents of the conversation we had in my dream. Days passed and at last, all the last rites were done. I eventually returned to the US and devoted myself to spiritual pursuits because I was convinced they would heal me.

I would like to share my spiritual breakthroughs from some of those pursuits before and after June 2020 as follows.

My Spiritual Insights and Breakthroughs

Over the years, I have experienced profound spiritual breakthroughs through deep work with my mind. One of my recent breakthroughs occurred during a solitary retreat, where I was left with only my thoughts to contend with. The environment allowed me to enter a hyper-focused state, from which I gained deep insights that would have been difficult to attain amid the distractions of daily life. While breakthroughs are possible at home, the practical constraints of family and society can get in the way. However, through regular spiritual practice, whether through devotion, service or knowledge, I have found that insights can come and breakthroughs can happen. This work is akin to altering one's mind or consciousness. I share my experiences not to boast but to encourage readers to pursue their own spiritual journeys, as breakthroughs can happen for anyone willing to put in the work. Following are some of the breakthroughs I have had over the years.

Breakthrough #1: Experience of *Krishna* and *Samadhi*, the Absorption in the Source

It was the spring of 2019. I remember being in the shower and listening to the *Chaap Tilak bhajan*, a devotional song, sung by Vinod Agarwal. I was crying profusely for Krishna (Krishna, a Hindu God, can also be interpreted as cosmic consciousness). My heart longed for one glimpse of him. The longing was so heart-wrenching that I had to duck down in the shower stall, holding my chest with both my hands. The lyrics of the bhajan, translated into English, mean something like this:

> The shining world with all its glory on one side and my bright *Shyam* (synonym for Krishna) on the other side . . . the good karma of several births has come to fruition that my beloved has become so dear to my heart. To take this birth and come to this world has become a success . . . The heart has become drunk in love with the dusky master. The divine nectar has reached its brim with the desire of having just one glimpse of the beloved.

I kept crying and calling for Krishna. I pined for him: *I have been continuously chanting your mantra for the last five years. Why can't I have a glimpse of you?* It was in 2014, in Rishikesh, that I was initiated into the Krishna Mantra and have been chanting it incessantly ever since.

When Krishna didn't respond to my prayers, I complained to the divine mother that her son was not listening to my pleas and had become stony-hearted. I felt light after crying for my beloved. It was almost like an emotional catharsis—we carry so many unresolved emotions within us; offering them back to God in some way often makes us feel lighter.

After I had my shower, I made my way to my meditation space to begin my afternoon practice. As I settled into my meditation chair, I felt a powerful presence, which I recognized as Krishna. Though my eyes were closed, I invited him to take a seat next to me. Strangely, he refused to sit down, prompting me to wonder why. Suddenly, I felt compelled to offer him my chair, and so I quietly moved to the other side of the chair and gestured for him to take my place. Despite my overwhelming desire to open my eyes and behold him, I remained afraid that doing so might cause him to vanish, and so I kept them tightly shut throughout the experience.

Once he took the seat, he guided me into a Self-inquiry meditation. He asked me to look for the Source where this sense of 'I' was rising from. Mentally dividing my body into smaller sections, I dived deep into each part to see if the sense of 'I' was rising from that part. When I reached my heart centre, something deeper sucked me into the Source. Only the light remained. Each and every pore of my body started vibrating with that golden light as if opening my pores for the merging with the ever-present divine. I experienced Extreme Bliss. I had never experienced anything like this before. Even if a hundred worlds with all their riches were offered to me, I wouldn't have traded a single moment of this divine experience. As I was experiencing this divine bliss, my heart filled with gratitude, and instead of falling deeper into the abyss of light, I tried to make an effort to come out and thank Krishna for making me experience this. I heard him say, 'NOT EVEN A FLICKER, STAY THERE!' and as if

by the force of his words, I fell into that abyss of light again.
I don't know how long I stayed there in that state, but when
I came out of my absorption, I had no sense of body. I tried
to move my hand and say to myself, 'This is my hand', but the
sense of *I* and *mine* was gone. I stayed in that state for almost
a month and then it slowly faded away.

Breakthrough #2: *Aparokshanubhuti* Contemplation, Realization of Oneness

Aparokshanubhuti, meaning direct Self-realization, is an
introductory text of the Vedanta. It was February 2020 and
I was listening to the forty-first Aparokshanubhuti lecture
of Swami Sarvapriyananda.* He was explaining the verse
pertaining to the four stages of pot and clay. The verse explains
that there is no outside world without Awareness (you can
think of Awareness as Cosmic Consciousness or God or
Universal Intelligence). Hence, the entire universe is nothing
but Awareness. The verse brings this point home with the
analogy of a pot and clay, where the pot is the experienced
world while the clay is analogous to Awareness, that is, the
cause of the effect which is the perceived world.

After listening to the lecture, I started with the process
of recollecting and contemplating the teachings. While I was
contemplating this teaching sitting in my meditation room,

---

* Swami Sarvapriyananda is a renowned Indian monk, Vedanta scholar
and spiritual teacher who currently serves as the minister and spiritual
leader of the Vedanta Society of New York, which is affiliated with the
Ramakrishna Order of India.

I focused on the wall in front of me. It had square blocks hanging on it. Going deep into contemplation, I started asking myself: Am I the Awareness, the material cause of this world? Is this world made of Awareness? Are these three square blocks made of 'I', the Awareness? If I were to remove the Awareness, would these blocks remain? I started to look deeper and, as if by magic, the blocks started shifting into the background and the Awareness started shining forth. When I looked around, everything seemed to give way to Awareness. I looked at my body, it seemed porous, as if it was merged with Awareness. Everything was the light of Awareness. Even the red traffic light that I encountered while driving later that day was bursting with Awareness. I wasn't able to locate my egoic self. I had merged with the universe.

Here is a note from that time: *I am not able to identify with the thoughts of this mind. I can watch all of them as they are rising and subsiding. Shweta feels like an inauthentic self. No inclination to do anything. Not able to sleep at night. While responding to other people, I have no reactions inside.*

I remember moving about and doing everything as if nobody was inside. At night, when I would close my eyes to try to fall asleep, a bright white light would appear as if somebody was pointing a glaring white torchlight at me. And when I would open my eyes, it would be completely dark outside. There was no sleep for me for three nights, as the same situation kept getting repeated. I didn't know whom to talk to or what to tell them regarding what was happening to me. I thought people might not understand it.

I prayed to God for assistance since I couldn't function in the world in that state. My prayers were answered. That evening, my husband was going out for a movie with his friend. I asked him if I could accompany him. We first stopped over at a friend's house where he served us chicken kebabs and other delicacies. Even though I had given up eating chicken years before, a voice from inside coaxed me into having it. We went to the movie theatre next. I think indulging in the worldly pleasures of eating meat and getting stimulated by the media finally broke the camel's back. I was pulled down from that high state and while Vishal and his friend watched the movie, I took a restful nap, finally!

Breakthrough #3: Emptiness and Experience of Luminosity

In the month of December, during a month-long solitary retreat, I was grappling with an unresolved mental pattern that kept pulling me into suffering. This pain had become almost tangible and was persistently haunting me. Having spent twenty-seven days at the retreat, I decided to take a closer look at this affliction. During my meditation session that day, I focused intently on my mind and began to inquire, starting with: '*Who is experiencing this pain?*' to which I received the answer, '*I*'. I continued with the next question, '*Who am I?*' and the answer came to me almost immediately—'*Shweta*'.

I resolved to investigate and have a closer look at 'Shweta'. During my meditation session, I focused intently on this question, asking myself who or what exactly Shweta was. I directed my mind to delve deeper and find the Source of this identity.

As I deliberated over this matter, I noticed within my mind these seeds of pain, pleasure, anger, gratitude and other emotions. Each seed seemed to contain various experiences, all made up of many words. These experiences were intertwined with my sense of self, creating a solid identity of 'Shweta'. However, as I examined each seed more closely, I realized that they were made up of nothing but fluff. By remaining present and focused, I was able to see through these experiences without forming an identity. Yet, when my attention waned, the identity of 'Shweta' resurfaced. So, I directed my attention to each and every seed until they were completely burnt. After going through this process for a long time, I couldn't find any concrete sense of self. So I asked myself: *Am I not really here? Is there nothing here?* And I was left with a very serene luminosity that was calming and expansive. When I opened my eyes, I saw that same luminosity pervading everything. I felt a deep sense of completion, my mind was completely peaceful, and I had discovered something that was eternal and ever-present. The world appeared like fiction, including this character of mine. What joy, what play! Tears of joy were rolling down my cheeks as I wrote down my meditation experience. Even now, that experience is readily available to me, and it is more real than the real.

Breakthrough #4: Experiencing Death Two-and-a-Half Times

It was March 2022, and I had just returned from my India trip. I had visited a lot of spiritual places like Rishikesh, Haridwar,

Varanasi, Vrindavan, Barsana, Belur Math (Kolkata) and Mayapur during the trip. It had been a surreal experience, from performing *Rudra Abhishek* to feeding the saints to dancing to the tunes of Krishna in Vrindavan.

But after I returned to the US, I started feeling restless. I would often feel dizzy, and my blood pressure shot up (my blood pressure is generally on the lower side). I was dealing with a lot of anxious thoughts, and though I was able to watch them, it was still taking a toll on my health. I talked to nurses and doctors and got every possible test done (I rarely see a doctor since I am a very healthy person). In that period of two or three months, I had a constant sense of restlessness, as if something was about to go wrong. My heart rate was faster than usual.

During this time, once when I was lying in bed at night, half-asleep, I experienced an intense fear of death rising. The feeling was so powerful it was almost visceral. I experienced it in the form of heat rising in my spinal column and intensifying when it reached the back of my neck. There was this liquid that seemed to be running through my spine, spreading all over my body and paralysing it. It produced an immense amount of panic and anxiety. I felt as if I were falling into an abyss, a total darkness gripping me. I was experiencing death at that moment, and my body was falling, paralysed by the amount of fear and liquid that were getting generated in my body. My blood pressure shot up to extremely high levels, my heart had never beaten faster, and I was covered in sweat. My mind was howling that this was death, I was dying and I wasn't able to control it. The fear of death and the unknown intensified the panic further. It was one of the most daunting and cataclysmic experiences of my life.

And without warning, I was subject to the same harrowing experience the very next night as well, albeit with a higher intensity. This time around, it was a double whammy since an extra layer of fear was added to it. The supplementary fear was the memory of the previous night's experience, reminding me that it had come back again and would make me suffer through hell. The experience was horrifying, to say the least. I lay there with the lower portion of my body paralysed. My heart was pulsating like a thunderbolt. I could hardly breathe and the fear of death had completely gripped me, pulling me to deeper and darker levels of my psyche than I had ever been before. I kept reminding myself to chant the name of God but nothing came to my rescue. I had to go through a complete cycle of facing death and experiencing it physically.

I was so scared of the experience that I didn't want to be left alone. My blood pressure was very high the next morning as well, and nothing felt good. I wanted a way out of this mess. I researched a lot online to figure out what was happening to me. Through all of this, I didn't let go of my mindfulness. I was highly aware of every passing thought and emotion.

Little did I know that it was all set to return the next night. As the feeling started rising in my spine, I became completely aware. I asked my mind to practise a sense of 'I Am-ness' and focus on its 'beingness' but somehow the fear in my mind gained momentum and started rising and spreading with fervour. It felt like a thud in my heart, *Oh, it has returned*. It drained me of whatever little courage I had. I was resisting the experience I was going through with all my might but the non-acceptance of the situation made me more restless. Eventually, I completely gave in and commanded myself to let go and experience whatever happens, since my years of spiritual practice informed me that it was all an illusion anyway. And to my surprise, the fear vanished never to return. That's why I call this the experience of death *two-and-a-half* times. This third experience was when the breakthrough of liberation from death happened.

* * *

These breakthrough experiences helped me resolve my trauma, whether it's from this life or previous ones (if you believe in reincarnation). Pain has the power to propel us towards growth and self-discovery, yet the search for the roots of our pain is also a journey of exploration. For it is in this process of discovery that we unravel the source of our suffering and find the key to unlocking our true potential. In the next chapter, we will discuss the sources of pain and how the pain can be used as a stepping stone to an awakened life.

1

The Pain of Losing and Living

'No mud, no lotus. Without suffering, there is no happiness. So we should not discriminate against the mud. We have to learn how to embrace and cradle our own suffering and the suffering of the world, with a lot of tenderness.'—Thich Nhat Hanh

Pain, in all its forms, can be our greatest teacher. It is by experiencing pain that we learn valuable lessons about ourselves and the world around us. However, handling and working through pain can be an arduous task that requires immense courage and unwavering commitment. It's tempting to shy away from pain, to bury it deep within ourselves and pretend it doesn't exist. After all, confronting pain means reliving the same agony and distress we felt the day the incident occurred.

But to truly find a solution to the problem of pain, we need to take a closer look at the problem itself. Let's explore the origins of pain and trauma, diving deep into topics such as childhood trauma, parenting, grief resulting from the loss of loved ones and the potential impact of pain on both our mental and physical health. By examining childhood trauma and parenting, we can begin to identify effective strategies for parenting that may help prevent some of the pain experienced by our children.

Certain types of trauma, such as the death of a loved one, are often unavoidable. In these instances, it becomes crucial to develop effective coping mechanisms that can help us navigate the aftermath of such events. In the final section of this chapter, we will discuss practical steps that can be taken to manage pain.

It's important to recognize that the price we pay for not healing from our pain is incredibly steep. When left unresolved, pain can fester within us and begin to affect our day-to-day lives. It can impact our relationships, our work and our overall sense of well-being. That's why it's imperative that we face our pain head-on and take the necessary steps to heal and move forward. Only then can we emerge stronger, wiser and more resilient than ever before.

Stored Trauma

Over the years, trauma has been heavily researched, and the data we've gathered provides us with a clearer understanding of this complex phenomenon. To begin, we must first grasp what trauma is at its core. At its essence, trauma is the lasting emotional response that our bodies and minds experience following an adverse event. It's crucial to acknowledge that the event itself does not define trauma. Everyone responds differently to situations, and what may be a traumatic experience for one person may not be so for another. Therefore, we should avoid comparing our traumatic events to determine who is holding on to more trauma within their systems. The temptation to compare our sufferings with those of others must be resisted. Each person's pain is valid and deserves to be treated with compassion and understanding.

Trauma is often measured using metrics, like Adverse Childhood Experiences (ACE), which assess the likelihood of developing mental and physical health issues from adverse events experienced in childhood. The more adverse events experienced, the higher the likelihood of trauma lingering in our bodies and minds.*

But this metric cannot predict the extent to which a person would have trauma stored in them because it cannot differentiate between the in-built resilience of different people. It also does not differentiate on the basis of the age at which a traumatic event takes place. Studies suggest that

---

* Felitti, V. J., Anda, R. F., Nordenberg, D., Williamson, D. F., Spitz, A. M., Edwards, V., . . . and Marks, J. S. (1998). Relationship of childhood abuse and household dysfunction to many of the leading causes of death in adults: The Adverse Childhood Experiences (ACE) Study. *American Journal of Preventive Medicine*, 14(4), 245–58.

This study conducted by the Centers for Disease Control and Prevention (CDC) and Kaiser Permanente found that adverse experiences in childhood, such as physical, emotional or sexual abuse, neglect and household dysfunction, were associated with a higher likelihood of experiencing negative health outcomes later in life. The study concluded that childhood trauma can have a long-lasting impact on physical and mental health, and the more adverse events encountered in childhood, the higher the likelihood of negative outcomes.

a difficult event at a younger age has a higher likelihood of translating into trauma than at a more mature age. The *ACE* questionnaire treats all ages under the age of eighteen equally and hence misses some important qualifiers. For instance, a child losing her parent at eight versus eighteen. While both are devastating, losing a parent at eight has more long-term disadvantages for the child and is likely to create more trauma inside her body.

There are other examples of how the first few years after a child's birth are critical in making sure that they don't retain long-term trauma. According to the *American Academy of Pediatrics*, trauma in infancy can alter the developing architecture of the brain. It can harm memory and executive functioning, in addition to learning capabilities. Hence, the stakes are pretty high but don't get captured in the ACE score.

Trauma expert Gabor Mate writes in his bestseller *The Myth of Normal* that there are two types of trauma: capital-T trauma and small-t trauma. Capital-T trauma occurs when bad things happen that shouldn't, like losing a parent early in life or experiencing child abuse or racism. This type of trauma can lead to mental or physical health issues such as inflammation and autoimmune disorders, lowering overall well-being.

Then there is small-t trauma. Small-t trauma is what is left behind in our systems, not because of some major traumatic events but because of smaller day-to-day events where our emotional and physical needs are not met. It can manifest from what *does not happen*. Let's say there is a sensitive child looking for warmth and affection from her parents. If the parents are not responsive, even though they are not abusive or neglectful, it could be stored in her little body as small-t trauma. Other events that could lead to small-t trauma are hurtful comments from otherwise caring parents or bullying by peers. These events are usually less memorable but their after-effects do manifest themselves later in life and interfere with the desire to be well-adjusted in society.

Since I don't want to keep distinguishing between the event and its effect, I want to introduce my readers to a new term coined by me for the sake of clarity—Stored Trauma.

Stored Trauma clarifies that what I am talking about is not the event itself but the trauma left behind in our bodies and minds due to the event. Stored Trauma rears its ugly head in our unconscious reactions to stressful situations. Stored Trauma sabotages our relationships and pushes us on paths we would not consciously choose. Stored Trauma is extremely important to understand and resolve. We will talk about how to resolve it in this book.

Childhood and Trauma

I chose the heading 'The Pain of Losing and Living' for this chapter to underscore the idea that although I went through the agony of losing several loved ones at a young age, there are numerous other sources of childhood trauma that can add to our anguish and hinder us from leading lives that are conscious and gratifying. Rather than blaming our parents or guardians, it's important to recognize the impact of these experiences so that we can begin the healing process. Research shows that acknowledging the roots of our suffering is key to finding peace and transformation. When healing happens, it changes our subconscious beliefs, but for the healing to happen, the conscious brain needs to be fully engaged. Healing is a process that takes time and comes with roadblocks and challenges. If our conscious brain is on board, it just makes the process easier because we can catch ourselves when operating from a space of Stored Trauma.

Also, trauma is often multi-generational. Mark Wolynn a leading expert in the field of inherited family trauma, talks about the lengthy chain of multigenerational trauma in his insightful book, *It Didn't Start with You: How Inherited Family Trauma Shapes Who We Are and How to End the Cycle.* This is another reason why blaming has no result. You will have to continue going back in time, eventually blaming evolution itself.

Pain and Illness

Since emotional pain and trauma are what happen inside us, they can have long-term effects on us. Before the bad news, I want to give you the good news. Since trauma is what has happened inside us and not to us, the damage is reversible and healing is possible. What happened to us (our environment) cannot be reversed but what happened inside us (mindset) can be reversed. This means the locus of control is internal and not external. Research shows that if we believe in an internal locus of control, we are more likely to be successful in any pursuit, including healing.* To put it simply, it is our mindset

---

* Wallston, K. A., Stein, M. J., and Smith, C. A. (1994). Form C of the MHLC scales: A condition-specific measure of locus of control. *Journal of Personality Assessment*, 63(3), 534–53.

and attitude towards situations that matter the most, not the situation itself.

Pivoting to the bad news: Stored Trauma can play havoc on our biology. This is not pseudoscience or mumbo jumbo. Many interviews and reports in the public domain highlight this oft-overlooked cause of our chronic diseases. Let's understand the biological mechanisms at play. The amygdala is considered the brain's fear centre. Higher stress has been correlated with higher activity in the amygdala, which is linked to higher chances of cardiovascular diseases. This is because higher amygdala activity causes increased bone marrow activity and inflammation of the arteries, leading to the heart-related ailments in question.

I don't want to bore you with an overwhelming amount of biology, but it's crucial to provide more examples to emphasize the link between trauma and illness. Ignoring this link could prevent millions from accessing the healing they need. While cancer is commonly understood as the growth of cancerous cells, many people have small amounts of these cells inside their bodies but do not develop the disease. However, stress can actually promote the growth of these cells by

---

This study examined the relationship between loci of control and health outcomes in patients with various medical conditions. The researchers found that patients who believed they had more control over their health and recovery (i.e., an internal locus of control) were more likely to engage in positive health behaviours and experience better outcomes. Conversely, patients who believed their health was beyond their control (i.e., an external locus of control) were less likely to play an active role in their recovery and had poorer outcomes.

releasing proteins that cause inflammation.* Unfortunately, these proteins impede healing mechanisms and worsen the problematic ones.† For instance, they can disable genes that fight tumour growth while enabling chemical messengers that support it.

Brain Science

Let's discuss the brain a bit more to understand the effects of stress better. I am no brain scientist and hence I will refer to one of my favourite books *Buddha's Brain: The Practical Neuroscience of Happiness, Love & Wisdom*, written by neuropsychologist Rick Hanson, in partnership with neurologist Richard Mendius. In it, the authors talk about the brain model proposed by the American physician and neuroscientist Paul MacLean. Called the *triune* brain model, it represents the brain in the form of three major layers of brain tissues that evolved in different eras.

The first layer, which includes the basal ganglia and the brain stem, is colloquially called the reptilian brain. It is the tissue complex that evolved first and is in charge of our primal instincts like aggression, dominance, territoriality and ritual displays. The basal ganglia are involved in motor skills,

---

* Thaker, P. H., Han, L. Y., Kamat, A. A., Arevalo, J. M., Takahashi, R., Lu, C., . . . and Sood, A. K. (2006). Chronic stress promotes tumour growth and angiogenesis in a mouse model of ovarian carcinoma. *Nature Medicine*, 12(8), 939–44.
† Segerstrom, S. C., and Miller, G. E. (2004). Psychological stress and the human immune system: A meta-analytic study of 30 years of inquiry. *Psychological Bulletin*, 130(4), 601–30.

while the brain stem regulates our blood pressure, sugar and respiration.

The complex which evolved next is called the Paleomammalian (*paleo* meaning old) brain and contains the limbic system. The limbic system includes the amygdala that we have spoken about and is responsible for emotions, motivation, learning, parenting and memory.

And the final complex, which evolved last, is called the Neomammalian (*neo* meaning new) brain and includes the neocortex. This complex enables abstract thinking, language, reasoning and planning. This is what Nobel Laureate Daniel Kahneman calls the slow brain. This is the part of the brain with which we make rational, informed decisions. It is supposed to be slow because rationality involves a lot of conscious information processing, in contrast with the lower areas of the brain that are fast and autonomous but operate at a more subconscious level.

Rick Hanson put it beautifully: 'Our brains are sponges for bad news and Teflon for good news.' The lower areas of the brain dominate our lives more than the prefrontal cortex (PFC), the part of the neocortex at the very front of the brain that plays a major role in inhibition and self-regulation. Thus, bad news gets more attention than good news because of evolution. In evolutionary terms, danger from a threat is more significant than the benefits of a positive experience. If our early ancestors had not paid attention to critical threats, they would not have been able to pass on their genes. Evolution encourages traits of survival, thus our brains perceive a threat more strongly than a positive experience. Humans have a predisposition to anxiety because of this reason.

And humans who have experienced traumatic events often cannot turn off their hypervigilant system in the reptilian and paleomammalian regions. This is manifested as constant stress and anxiety in their bodies.

From Thinking to Doing to Becoming

The good news is that we can wire our brains for health, happiness and well-being. We can change some aspects of our biology by thought alone. To put it in simple words, we can exercise mind over matter.

The neocortex, the limbic brain and the reptilian brain allow us to accomplish multiple functions—from thinking to doing to becoming. The seat of the conscious mind, the neocortex, helps in analysing and processing given information. Once it has completely analysed the information as true and helpful, we can train our limbic brain to accept and integrate the idea through the corresponding emotions, since our limbic system learns through feelings and emotions.

For example, let us take a situation where we learn that anger causes more harm to our bodies than to the person whom we are angry with. We analyse this knowledge further by researching it. In the process, we find out how anger triggers the fight or flight response in our bodies, thus releasing stress hormones like cortisol and adrenaline. The body prepares by increasing the blood pressure, respiration and heart rate, and they in turn increase our body temperature and perspiration. Unmanaged anger has a long-lasting harmful impact on different organs of our body as it generates and releases stress chemicals constantly into the bloodstream with the accompanying metabolic changes.

After being completely convinced that anger causes more harm to our own bodies and works like poison in our bodies, we can train our limbic brain to integrate this information. We can do this by storing a visual in our mind to invoke a certain emotion. So, for example, in the case of training our minds that anger is bad for our health, we can save a visual of holding a burning coal in our hands and waiting to throw it at the person who we think has made us angry. Now, every time we are in a situation where we feel that anger rising, we can bring this vision to our mind. This, in turn, will invoke the emotion of caution and wisdom that anger does more harm to us than the person we are angry with. Indeed, being angry isn't good for anybody, not for us and not for the person we are angry with. If we culture our mind to this information by practising this association every time a similar situation arises, we are priming our subconscious or our reptilian brain. Being calm in the midst of anger-inducing circumstances becomes our innate personality trait. We go from thinking that anger is harmful, to practising mindful restraints when anger arises to becoming calm and wise. That's how wisdom is integrated or sinks into the subconscious and becomes part of who we are. It is all about thinking, doing and becoming. It takes time but we get there eventually.

Epigenetics

Our body is our manifested subconscious. The more our subconscious is primed with wisdom, the fewer blockages or diseases our bodies will manifest. Let us try and understand the connection between our subconscious mind and our physical body through the lens of epigenetics.

The Greek prefix *epi* in 'epigenetics' means over, outside of or around, implying that the word epigenetics refers to features that are in addition to or on top of the traditional genetic basis for inheritance. Traditionally, it was believed that our genes determined our physical bodies, minds and behaviours. However, *epigenetics* suggests that whether those genes are turned on or off depends on the environment. A certain gene might be present in the parent but not turned on. The same gene present in the child could get turned on based on the child's early childhood environment. The flip side of the coin is that the gene could be turned on in the parent and the parent could pass on the turned-on gene to the child. But the child's environment could turn off the gene. The point here is that environment is of the essence.

Our DNA (that contains genetic information and lives inside the cell) is controlled by signals outside the cell, including the energy from our positive or negative thoughts. Thought (conscious or subconscious) leads to neural activity and neural activity interacts with the DNA via the cell membrane of the cell. If there are a lot of negative thoughts and memories stored in the subconscious, they will keep emanating neural energy, leading to the turning on of genes responsible for ill health and sickness.* On the other hand, if the subconscious

---

* Tyrka, A. R., Price, L. H., Marsit, C., Walters, O. C., and Carpenter, L. L. (2012). Childhood adversity and epigenetic modulation of the leukocyte glucocorticoid receptor: preliminary findings in healthy adults. *Journal of Psychiatric Research*, 46(9), 910–16.

is full of positive reinforcement, it could potentially turn off sickness-causing genes. This applies to conscious thoughts as well but our subconscious patterns sometimes get the better of the conscious. If the core beliefs stored in our subconscious (about our self-worth or capability) are limiting, it is hard to change those with conscious thought. The trick here is to catch the negative subconscious thoughts and transform them into positive conscious thoughts. With time and practice, those negative subconscious thoughts will be replaced by positive ones because the neural pathways (how we learn) for those positive thoughts will become stronger and stronger each time we practise this exercise. This, however, is easier said than done and you need strong conviction and a diligent attitude to transform and heal. It involves dedicated practice and a commitment to reprogramming the subconscious.

The concept of kinesiology also highlights the power of the subconscious mind and exhibits the mind–body connection. Kinesiology is the scientific study of human body movement. One of the applications of kinesiology is muscle testing. This process involves answering questions or saying statements out loud. If there is a conflict between the conscious answer/ statement and a subconsciously held belief, it will show up

---

In this study, researchers examined the relationship between childhood trauma, negative thoughts and emotions and DNA methylation of the glucocorticoid receptor (GR) gene, which is involved in the regulation of the stress response. They found that individuals who reported more negative thoughts and emotions had higher levels of DNA methylation of the GR gene, and that this increased methylation was associated with an increased risk of developing depression. These findings suggest that negative thoughts and emotions can contribute to epigenetic changes that increase the risk of developing mental health problems.

as a weakening of body muscles. A famous study involves keeping your arms raised in front of you (making a 90-degree angle with your body) while the examiner asks you to say: 'I am *<someone else's name>*' while applying downward pressure on your arms. Your muscles will weaken and your arms will be depressed with the examiner's applied pressure. On the contrary, when you say your own name, you will be able to resist the examiner's applied pressure easily.

Now that we know the subconscious has so much power over us, we must find ways of exerting conscious control over it. One interesting way to prove that the conscious can eventually conquer the subconscious is the method of biofeedback. As we discussed earlier, most of our autonomic functions like body temperature, blood pressure and heart rate are managed by our subconscious brain system. Biofeedback is a type of mind–body technique you use to control some of your body's functions, such as your heart rate, breathing patterns and muscle responses.

I once talked to Akshay Vinod Shukla, a reporter from the Television Channel TV9, to understand how a *yogi* can control these autonomic systems using conscious yogic techniques. Akshay had followed a yogi called Ish Putra, the present head of *Kaulantak Peeth*, into the Himalayas. While Akshay and his crew were heavily clothed and protected with the modern world's technology to combat sub-zero temperatures, the yogi went about his business barefoot and bare-chested in the snow, going deep into the mountains and stopping at places to meditate. I wanted to confirm the veracity of the report I had seen on a TV9 segment. Akshay explained that all of it was accurate. They had been worried that if something happened to the yogi on national television, the channel could be sued for endangering human life or not protecting the yogi. However, the yogi didn't show any signs of trouble and even climbed an extremely tall deodar tree and meditated atop it. They had to send drones out to capture footage of how high above the earth the yogi was meditating.

The point here is that the yogi was able to manage his body temperature using the yogic techniques he had consciously learned over the years. This is a triumph of the conscious over the subconscious. Even ordinary humans like us can use biofeedback to master our autonomous systems.

If we can consciously exert mastery over our innate functions, it is certainly possible to reprogram our subconscious to remove negative and self-limiting beliefs. To be able to consciously control the subconscious, one needs to undergo extensive training and commit to hard work. It is only then that you can potentially heal from the trauma you have encountered in your life.

However, not everyone has equal access to this knowledge and training. Moreover, despite the potential for healing, not everyone can benefit from it. Thus, it is better to prevent exposure to avoidable trauma and unhealthy subconscious programming to begin with. In addition to training our own subconscious, we must also be mindful of our parenting practices to avoid passing on unresolved patterns to the next generation. Effective conscious parenting can have a significant impact in reducing the need for later subconscious retraining. In short, it's easier to prevent the damage than to try and fix it later.

Parenting Consciously and Raising Resilient Children

One of the ways that adults can use this knowledge of the power of the subconscious mind and how it can affect our lives is by choosing conscious parenting. Research on electroencephalograms (EEGs), which measure the brain's fluctuating electrical activity, divides the dominant frequencies at which brains operate in humans into different age groups. From birth until two years of age, EEGs record mostly the lowest EEG frequency called the delta waves. As we progress in age, until six years of age, brain activity is dominated by higher frequency theta waves. This is followed by alpha waves until the age of twelve and then beta waves in adolescence and adulthood. A new EEG frequency called gamma waves has also been identified, which exhibits itself when the subject is performing at their peak or experiencing a state of flow (a state of optimal experience), as coined by the Hungarian–American psychologist Mihaly Csikszentmihalyi. The main characteristics of beta waves are activity and focus, while the main characteristics of alpha waves are calm consciousness and a sense of self. However, it is the delta and theta waves that put the brain in the most suggestive state, priming it to absorb environmental messages like a sponge and to store them in the subconscious to form the fast brain. This is why young children in the first few years of their lives are more likely to pick up a new language easily while it takes far more effort in later years. These programmable years are extremely important from a parent's perspective. If we plant positive self-beliefs, resilience and a growth mindset in these early years, it will form a strong foundation for our child's subconscious brain but if we do it the other way around, it will take our child a long time to undo the damage. This is also our opportunity to inculcate faith and prayer in our children. While we cannot control what circumstances our children will face in their lives, we can arm them with the tools they would need to stay resilient in the face of hardships. Faith and prayer can act as an armour in such situations.

Parents should try their best to nurture their children's subconscious with positive affirmations and beliefs. There are three mechanisms through which parents pass on characteristics to their children. The first is the most widely understood method of genetics (the transfer of general physical characteristics and genetic material). The second is what we have discussed previously—epigenetics, where the parents can pass on the turned-on-off combination of their genes to their children, based on their own life experiences. This is akin to saying that while children do not necessarily inherit all the behavioural and physiological characteristics of parents, they do inherit some combination of their parents' nervous systems (on-off combinations). This is why some kids are more sensitive than others, starting from birth. The third is the environment the parents provide to the child. This is what the parents have control over. This also plays into epigenetics. The environment can build the core subconscious brain of the child, which exerts a strong influence over the child's future behaviour and attitude. In addition, the environment and the subconscious brain built with it can turn gene activity on or off over the long term, having a great influence on a child's mental and physical health. If all goes well, children thrive and develop into well-adjusted adults with a growth mindset. If parents are not able to provide a healthy environment for their children, they could end up developing some unhealthy coping mechanisms.

Coping Mechanisms

Coping mechanisms are the techniques and behaviours we adopt to manage the challenges and difficulties we encounter in our lives. They are often learned behaviours that aim to reduce anxiety and distress in the short term. They can be conscious or unconscious, and are shaped by our experiences and surroundings. Coping mechanisms can arise in response to traumatic or adverse events, and can be positive or negative in nature.

Dr Gabor Mate explains that coping mechanisms can cause significant stress because they involve a conflict between authenticity and attachment. When the attachment in relationships is insecure, people are not as authentic and vulnerable because they are afraid that their authenticity might lead to rejection. Hence, for the sake of attachment, they sacrifice authenticity. If our emotional needs are not met during childhood, we may adjust our behaviour to fit the situation, leading us to adopt coping mechanisms that deny our pain. As adults, these mechanisms may persist and result in unfulfilled needs within our relationships.

For example, if parents consistently rely on their child to fulfil their own needs, the child may become overly responsible and self-sacrificing, suppressing their own emotional needs and suffering internal stress. In more severe cases, if a parent is abusive or unable to protect their child, the child may develop coping mechanisms such as extreme self-sufficiency or even rebellion and violence, leading to further stress and conflict.

Coping mechanisms can take many forms and vary in intensity and duration. Some may be functional and healthy, while others may be maladaptive and harmful. Some examples of maladaptive coping mechanisms include substance abuse to numb emotional pain or avoid reality, which can lead to addiction and other problems. Avoidance of situations or people that trigger negative emotions or memories can also be maladaptive, leading to isolation and missed opportunities for personal growth.

On the other hand, adaptive coping mechanisms, such as mindfulness, exercise or creative expression, can be effective in managing stress and regulating emotions in a positive way. Practising mindfulness meditation can help us become more aware of our thoughts and emotions, and develop greater acceptance and a non-judgemental attitude. Regular exercise can also improve our mood and reduce stress, promoting better physical and mental health.

Developing Conscious Coping Mechanisms

Developing conscious coping mechanisms involves becoming aware of our current coping strategies and evaluating whether they are effective and healthy. Here are some steps to develop conscious coping mechanisms:

- Identify your current coping mechanisms: Start by reflecting on how you typically cope with stress and emotional pain. Do you tend to avoid difficult situations, distract yourself with activities or substances, seek support from others or something else?

- Evaluate the effectiveness of your coping mechanisms: Consider whether your coping mechanisms are effective in reducing stress and promoting well-being in the long term. Do they help you solve problems and manage your emotions, or do they only provide temporary relief? Are they helping you reach your goals or are they holding you back?

- Assess the healthiness of your coping mechanisms: Consider whether your coping mechanisms are healthy and sustainable in the long term. Are they harming your physical or mental health or creating additional problems? Are they causing harm to others or straining your relationships?

- Identify alternative coping mechanisms: Consider healthier, more effective coping mechanisms that align with your values and goals. Some examples may include mindfulness, exercise, creative expression or seeking professional support. Experiment with different coping mechanisms and see what works best for you.

- Practise conscious coping: As you identify and experiment with new coping mechanisms, make a conscious effort to integrate them into your daily routine. Make a commitment to practising healthy coping mechanisms consistently, even when you're not feeling particularly stressed or overwhelmed.

In order to manage stress and emotional pain in a healthy and sustainable way, it's important to develop conscious coping mechanisms. This is a process that requires time and effort, as well as a willingness to learn and grow. Seeking support from friends, family or professionals can be helpful in this journey, as can practising self-compassion and patience. By consciously choosing coping mechanisms that are adaptive and healthy, we can create a more fulfilling and balanced life for ourselves.

Stories that Tell

After exploring the connection between trauma, stress and ill health, I am drawn to share stories that illustrate this relationship. One example is the story of Anita Moorjani, a woman known for her book and TEDx talk titled 'Dying To Be Me'. Anita was diagnosed with lymphoma, a type of cancer. While her Near Death Experience (NDE) is one dimension to her story, I will focus more on her overall story of developing coping mechanisms. Her personality before she was diagnosed with lymphoma was that of a compulsive people pleaser, extremely self-denying and self-sacrificing. Only in the face of cancer did she understand this tension within her, the deep desire to fulfil her own needs, competing against the coping mechanism to go along with everyone else's needs at the expense of her own. This realization, combined with conventional medical treatments, was the key to her recovery. Experts suggest that had she not addressed her emotional and physical needs, medical intervention alone would not have been enough to cure her. As I mentioned earlier, stress can fuel the spread of cancer, making it even more crucial to develop healthy coping mechanisms.

The second story is a little different. It focuses on another coping mechanism, that of self-destruction. Eve Ensler, popularly recognised as V, is known for her play *The Vagina Monologues*. However, the more important story here is her trauma from the sexual abuse at the hands of her father. She writes in her book *In the Body of the World: A Memoir of Cancer and Connection* about how her encounter with uterine cancer eventually led to her understanding of the trauma she had been harbouring in her body from the recurring abuse from the age of five to ten. She openly discusses her dependence on drugs and alcohol and other self-destructive habits. Ensler reveals that her experience with cancer forced her to confront the trauma that she had buried deep within herself and how her behaviour was adding to her pain. She writes, 'I finally realized that I was punishing myself for something that wasn't my fault.' Her coping mechanism of self-destruction was a way to numb the pain that she had been carrying for years. Through meditation practices, therapy and connecting with other survivors of sexual abuse, Ensler was able to find a way to confront and heal from her trauma. She writes, 'I began to see my cancer as a gift, an opportunity to finally face my demons and heal from the inside out.' Ensler's story shows us that while coping mechanisms may provide temporary relief, they can also prevent us from truly healing from our traumas. It takes courage to confront the pain that we have been carrying for so long, but it is necessary to move forward and live a wholesome life.

The third story is the most transformative one. It is the story of the one and only—Oprah Winfrey. Oprah details her abuse at the hands of her grandmother while growing up, in her book *What Happened to You?* Her coping mechanism was to become a world-class people-pleaser. She also talks in detail about her difficult relationship with her mother. Oprah lived with her grandmother in her early years. At age six, she was sent to her mother in Milwaukee. Her mother worked as a maid back then and was living with a very light-skinned black woman, who could pass for white. This other woman took an instant dislike to the dark-skinned six-year-old, highlighting how prejudiced we humans are even within our own racial and religious groups. She used to order Oprah to sleep on the porch, instead of inside the house with her mother. And her mother didn't question the order and asked Oprah to comply with the command. Imagine a little six-year-old girl, separated from her mother and sleeping outside the house by herself. What must be going on in her heart and mind? She must have felt rejected and abandoned by her own mother. Oprah recalls that it was her faith and belief in a higher power that helped her get through those tough times. She was afraid but she believed that God was with her. Quoting her, 'I remember praying on my knees the very first night I had been removed from my grandmother. I don't remember ever shedding a tear about it because I knew that God was my father, Jesus was my brother, and they were with me.'

Towards the end of the aforementioned book, she recounts an incident related to her mother's passing. Her mother passed away on 22 November 2018, Thanksgiving Day. In the days before her death, Oprah would go and sit beside her hospital bed and talk to her. She would read to her but was unable to tell her what she had always wanted to. On one of these nights, after failing again to utter the unsaid words, she left the hospital for a public-speaking gig. She wondered if her audience on television knew her better than her mother. It was ironic that the great public speaker, en route to a public speaking engagement, was unable to speak her heart out to her own mother. That night, she turned around and decided that the unsaid words had to be said and the inevitable had to be reckoned with. She went back to the hospital bed but the words still eluded her. She started singing and praying with her mother and that's when the breakthrough happened. She finally opened up and talked to her mother. She told her that she forgave her, that she had forgiven her a very long time ago. She told her that she understood that she must have been a scared, young woman when she got pregnant but still kept the baby instead of getting her aborted. She reassured her that she understood that she did her best, given her circumstances. That was a watershed moment for Oprah— to say something that she had never found the courage to say earlier. This also demonstrates my earlier point about how blaming your parents will not help you heal. It's the forgiveness that helps you heal.

Look at Oprah's life. She has successfully conquered a lot of her trauma and is actively involved in healing others with similar trauma. Her story is a great example of the true transformation of pain into something magical.

There are so many stories of people who have self-healed after resolving their psychological problems. One should take inspiration from the stories of Oprah Winfrey, Eve Ensler,

Anita Moorjani and Louise Hay.* These stories show us that we can heal ourselves.

Grief

In addition to the impact of trauma on the body, I would like to highlight the effects of grief. Although it may not be as widely discussed, I believe that grief is another form of trauma that can be equally damaging. The loss of a loved one can have a significant impact on the body, as evidenced by research showing that parents who lose adult sons to accidents or military conflicts are more likely to develop various types of cancer. I personally witnessed this when my father underwent bypass surgery after the death of my brother, Sushant, which was undoubtedly heartbreaking for him in the most literal sense. This illustrates how grief can exacerbate existing physical ailments or even lead to the development of new ones. Grief, its psychological effects, the immune system and the nervous system are all interconnected.

Grief is personally very significant to me because the major trauma I have harboured in my life has been from the pain of losing my loved ones.

---

* A famous author, she was diagnosed with a supposedly incurable form of cervical cancer. She concluded that cancer had manifested itself because of the resentment (stored trauma in our parlance) she was harbouring. She began a different regimen of healing that involved forgiveness, nutrition and reflexology in addition to therapy. Hay was able to heal herself with these methods. She transmuted her pain into healing.

Types of Grief

Research shows that there are two kinds of grief—uncomplicated and complicated. Uncomplicated grief is the preferred one; it usually leads to growth and development. According to *The Merck Manual*, which details information on various diseases, disorders and medical conditions, uncomplicated grief might still manifest as 'anxiety symptoms such as initial insomnia, restlessness, autonomic nervous system hyperactivity', but does 'not generally cause clinical depression, except in those persons inclined to mood disorder'. The complicated type is the one that we don't want. The complicated type is what is also called pathological bereavement. One of the conditions for pathological bereavement is when the survivor and the deceased are unusually dependent on each other.

Amongst all the causes of grief, the grief of losing a parent has been well-studied. What do you think the loss of a parent is in most cases? In most cases, it is the complicated type.* One of the questions usually asked† to understand if grief is of the complicated type is this: Was the bereaved actually very dependent upon the deceased person for pleasure, support or

---

* Prigerson, H. G., Horowitz, M. J., Jacobs, S. C., Parkes, C. M., Aslan, M., Goodkin, K., . . . and Maciejewski, P. K. (2009). Prolonged grief disorder: Psychometric validation of criteria proposed for DSM-V and ICD-11. *PLoS Medicine*, 6(8), e1000121.

In this study, the authors state that 'The most commonly experienced loss was the death of a parent (38%), followed by spouse/partner (22%), and child (15%). Consistent with prior reports, losing a parent was more frequently associated with complicated grief than losing a spouse/partner or child.' (p. 3).

† Diagnostic criteria suggested by David Peretz, M.D., of the Department of Psychiatry at Columbia University.

esteem? When I lost my mother, I was barely an adult, I had just turned eighteen. I was certainly dependent on her, not so much for pleasure, but for support and esteem. The other question is: did the bereaved feel helpless without the lost person when enforced separations occurred? This one is harder for me to agree to. I did not feel helpless but I was heartbroken.

Overall, my grief at losing my mother was the uncomplicated type, perhaps because I was a bit more mature when she passed away, compared to those who lose their parents earlier in life. Her death eventually led to growth and development, though it created a lot of turbulence inside me in the process.

Physiological and Psychological Reactions to Grief

The physiological effects of the stored trauma from grief have been seen in animals, birds and humans alike. Dolphins refuse to eat when their mate dies. Geese fly around, calling and searching, getting disoriented and lost in the process. Humans also stop eating and don't breathe properly. They get ear infections and clog their sinuses with the tears they haven't shed. Cognition falls and mortality increases. One study suggests that if you don't have a life partner and are struck with bereavement, you are more likely to die compared to folks who have partners.* This could be because of not having physical and emotional comfort during a time of

---

* Christakis, N. A., and Iwashyna, T. J. (2003). The health impact of health care on families: a matched cohort study of hospice use by decedents and mortality outcomes in surviving, widowed spouses. *Social Science & Medicine*, 57(3), 465–75.

physiological and psychological upheaval. As I mentioned in the introduction of this book, I suffered from a feeling of suffocation and sleep paralysis around the time of my mother's death.

When a loved one dies, family members and friends feel abandoned. Grief from such an event comes in waves, sudden psychological realizations of being left behind and of loss. These waves also manifest as bodily reactions like 'a feeling of tightness in the throat, choking with shortness of breath, need for sighing, and an empty feeling in the abdomen, lack of muscular power, and an intense subjective distress described as tension and mental pain.'*

Melanie Klein, an Austrian-British psychoanalyst, in her 1940 book *Mourning and Its Relation to Manic-Depressive States* writes at length about the psychological effects of grief. 'The mourner is in fact ill, but because this state of mind is common and seems so natural to us, we don't call mourning an illness . . . To put my conclusion more precisely: I should say that in mourning, the subject goes through a modified and transitory manic-depressive state and overcomes it.'

The Vortex Effect of Grief

The Vortex Effect is similar to the waves I talked about in the previous section. However, one difference is that it is brought about by association with places and things. More nostalgic in nature, it occurs when you come across places and things

---

* Quoted in a 1944 study by Eric Lindemann, who was the chief of psychiatry at Massachusetts General Hospital in the 1940s.

you associate with the loss. The Vortex Effect used to strike me very hard on my trips back home to Patna—the streets where mom and I went on morning walks, the rooms where we shared affection, the kitchen where she cooked her famous fish recipes, all those places sucked me into that vortex of nostalgia and loss. Even today, when I grab one of my old diaries in California, it takes me back to my mother, just by association.

The Stages of Grief

Psychiatrist Elisabeth Kubler-Ross's seven stages of grief is the most established model to understand how people grieve. The stages are as follows: shock, denial, anger, bargaining, depression, testing and acceptance. The process is not linear and people move in and out of different stages at different times. The end goal, however, is acceptance, along with growth and development.

I went through these stages more vividly after my brother Sushant's death than after my mother's. Maybe I was more mature at the time I lost him and hence I could discern better which stage of grief I experienced when and why.

In the next section, I will discuss what helps in dealing with grief and what worked for me in those times of turbulence.

Losing a Loved One—the Greatest Pain

How does the death of a loved one feel? The death of a loved one is a pain that seeps into every aspect of your being. It feels like a deep wound that will never fully heal. After Sushant's passing, I felt as if I was walking on thin ice, afraid that at any moment, the ground would give way beneath me. Our family, once seemingly unbreakable, now felt like a delicate vase that had been shattered into a million fragments. The loss of Sushant had left us all feeling fragile and vulnerable, struggling to pick up the pieces and move forward. Sushant's absence left a void that seemed impossible to fill.

The cruel reality of death becomes painfully evident when we lose someone dear to us. The pain that we won't be able to see their physical form again, look in their eyes, see their smile, touch them, hold and kiss them. Never again will these come to pass. The thought tears our hearts apart and makes us feel the pain we have never felt before. The memories we have shared haunt us. We crave to relive those moments again, maybe with more presence and with complete attention to the loved one we are missing. How much do we wish to turn back time or undo death! It almost feels like a nightmare, but one that we will never wake up from and the pain keeps growing deeper and deeper. To recover from such grief feels impossible.

There were so many moments that felt incomplete without Sushant. The holidays were not the same. The laughter was not as hearty. The memories were bittersweet. I felt like I was missing a part of myself. The thought of never seeing him again, never hearing his voice or feeling his embrace, was a pain that consumed me. It was like a part of my heart had been ripped away, leaving a wound that never fully healed. It was as though a vital piece of me was missing a limb that I could never regain.

The pain of losing a loved one is magnified when it's not a natural death. The questions and doubts that come with it are like a constant ache. *Could I have done more? Could I have saved them?* It's a pain that never fades, but instead ebbs and flows, like a turbulent ocean. And as the waves of grief crash over you, you realize that life will never be the same again.

Dealing with the Pain—the Doom's Way and the Effective Way

The Doom's Way

The doom's way is not the suggested way to deal with loss. In this way, we allow ourselves to be consumed by psychological pain. It is almost like finding a reason to remain unhappy for the rest of our lives. We keep harping on the past, get mired in regret and, most of all, do not accept what has already happened. This creates resistance in our psyche that doesn't allow us to be comfortable with the present moment. The constant struggle reflects on our mental and physical health. It leaves us drained, with no energy to even carry out our day-to-day chores. Sooner or later, we feel victimized and grow sour towards life.

This way should be completely avoided. Our gloominess will not only affect us but also those around us. We pay a heavy price if we don't heal from the pain. The unresolved pain is pushed to our subconscious mind and starts affecting our day-to-day life.

Road Map to the Effective Way

Coping with grief can feel like a daunting task, one that requires a tremendous amount of effort and energy. It's easy to feel like we're fighting an uphill battle against the pain, but it's important to remember that healing is a process that takes time. It's okay to not be okay, and instead of trying to suppress or fight our pain, we must allow ourselves to feel it fully. Every tear shed and every emotion felt is a vital component of the healing process.

Despite how difficult it may be, we can choose to approach pain differently. Rather than simply enduring it, we can consciously transmute it into something beautiful. We've been conditioned to avoid pain, but by embracing it, we can uncover hidden truths about ourselves and our place in the world. Pain can be a catalyst for profound spiritual growth and self-discovery, connecting us to our deeper selves and to the universe at large. By allowing ourselves to experience the pain and work through it, we can come out on the other side with a new-found strength and perspective. Pain teaches us to appreciate life and the people in it more, knowing just how precious and fleeting all of it is. This shift can be described as moving from brain-drain to brain-train, where we use our pain as an opportunity for growth and development.

Now, what do I mean when I say 'brain-drain'?

When I talk about brain-drain, I'm not referring to the typical *brain-drain* where countries lose their talented individuals to other countries. Instead, I'm using the analogy of a laptop or cell phone battery getting drained out because of many applications running. Unresolved pain or issues are like these running or open apps, draining our mental battery until we address them and close them one by one. When we fail to process our grief and distract ourselves with other activities, we are essentially pushing our unprocessed emotions and thoughts to our subconscious, which drains our mental energy. This can leave us feeling exhausted, leading us to rely on substances like caffeine and other stimulants to keep us going. We caffeinate ourselves to get the daily work done and then we numb ourselves by taking alcohol to calm our nerves, becoming highly dependent on external substances in the process. However, these external crutches only provide temporary relief and can lead to further problems.

So we must go from brain-drain to brain-train. Now, what is 'brain-train'?

It essentially means shifting our focus from avoiding our unresolved pain to actively addressing it. Instead of distracting ourselves with external stimuli, we must gather the strength and courage to face our pain head-on. This process requires patience, self-compassion and a willingness to sit with ourselves and let our minds bring up every unresolved issue that is draining our energy. Our subconscious mind knows which files are open, and when we are ready, it will bring them to our conscious mind to be resolved one by one. Meditation can be a powerful tool in this process, as it triggers the subconscious mind to send these files to our conscious mind for processing. By engaging in this brain-train process, we can free ourselves from the draining effects of unresolved pain and move towards a healthier and more energized life.

The key is to approach pain with mindfulness, acceptance and surrender. The idea is to let the pain transform us positively—think of it as channelling our inner *Shiva*. The Hindu God's consumption of the poison produced during *samudra manthan* and his mindful storage of it in his throat centre, without being affected by it, serves as a powerful metaphor for how we can deal with pain. *Samudra manthan* or the churning of the ocean is an excellent analogy for our lives. Just as many things were produced during the churning of the ocean, our life situations can range from auspicious and positive events to relatively sour and negative ones. To achieve the best possible outcome, we need to prevent negativity from spreading or, even better, transform it into something good, much like Shiva with the poison.

A moth's metamorphosis into a butterfly involves shedding its old identity and embracing the unknown, a painful yet necessary process. Similarly, resisting the natural course of pain can only cause more suffering. It's essential to accept and surrender to pain, just like the moth surrenders to nature's force. Likewise, a diamond's formation is the result of tremendous pressure and heat, a transformation of coal into a shining jewel. This process reminds us that discomfort and pain are necessary for growth and transformation. Just as a moth embraces the force of nature to become a beautiful butterfly and carbon endures immense pressure and heat to become a dazzling diamond, we too must surrender to the transformative power of pain within us.

Pain—the Portal to Enlightenment

Can pain be a portal to enlightenment? Yes, we can be alchemists; we can change base metal into gold. If pain is seen as an opportunity that can push us to get awakened, then pain has truly played its part. Don't see pain as something you want to run away from. It is a part of life and should be accepted wholeheartedly.

When a surge of pain arises in the body and wrenches your heart, become totally present. Be interested in it, watch it, and see what it feels like. It is just an emotion arising in you at the moment and it will eventually pass, as all emotions do. Watch every thought that rises in your mind related to that particular pain sensation, how these thoughts are feeding the pain and how this pain in turn generates more such thoughts in the mind. It is a feedback loop in which thoughts feed the pain and the pain in turn feeds the thoughts.

The unpleasantness of the pain produces fear, a fear of sitting and experiencing the discomfort of the pain. That energy of fear doesn't let us process the pain; it keeps us on the go and we find ourselves busier than ever before. Pain and fear are deeply intertwined. We even begin to fear anticipated pain. For example, if we are having an emotional breakdown today, and we are intensely missing our loved ones and our heart seems to sink, our mind will project that we will never come out of this state. Our mind projects and imagines painful and fearful incidents and keeps us under the impression that they are endless.

Breaking away from this pattern of thinking is crucial. This continuous loop of fear and pain can result in anxiety and panic attacks, preventing us from being in the present moment where true healing can occur. Instead of being caught up in the movement of fear and pain, we must learn to unclench and relax into the 'Now'. This is not just some mystical concept— it means being entirely mindful of our actions in the present moment, no matter what we are doing. Whether we are slicing vegetables, taking a stroll or even taking a shower, we must intentionally slow down and be present. Simultaneously, we should be conscious of any thoughts passing through our minds. This requires effort and grit, but with time, it gets easier and starts generating joy as we get habituated to getting into a flow state by practice.

The Way Out Is Turning In

One day in the morning during a solitary retreat, after two-and-a-half hours of meditation, I started feeling sick to my stomach because of the traumas and unconscious patterns I had personally lived through. It was a gut-wrenching feeling to the point of purging. I decided to write down my thoughts in a journal, pouring them all out. I remember being completely mindful, intensely and acutely present with my feelings, so much so that I kept weeping all through the process of writing. I was kind and gentle with myself and with the people who came to my mind who I thought had done me wrong. I didn't judge or blame myself or the other people but I keenly observed the unconscious patterns that govern the psyche. I observed how greed, jealousy, selfishness and anger take root in an unobserved mind and how they play with one's well-being. Not blaming or owning any of these defilements was the key; I merely observed them without judgement. I sat for meditation after writing and deeply witnessed the cause of these unconscious patterns. This contemplation led to a beautiful insight.

My complaints and thoughts were a result of conscious and unconscious patterns inherited from our ancestors, I surmised. Reflecting on my lineage, I envisioned my great-grandmother bravely encountering a snake and responding with compassion and love, a valuable lesson that had been transmitted through both genetics and teachings. However, I also realized that the fear and pain she may have experienced from a fire that left her crippled had been transmitted through generations as unresolved trauma. Our ancestors live on in us, and their learning process continues through our bodies. As their continuation, we carry on this process until defilements are completely dissolved through full enlightenment.

We are not as separate as we consider ourselves to be. This realization only leads to more compassion for our parents, our grandparents and our whole lineage. The sense of boundary, of solitary individuality goes away and the truth is seen in its most innate form. Any kind of arrogance or self-pity dissolves through this insight. A sense of connection and continuation is established.

When we work on healing ourselves in the present, we heal our past and our ancestors from the wounds that run deep in our family. When we heal our ancestors, we heal the human race from generations of idiosyncrasies, and we heal the world at large. Working on healing yourself is not only an act of courage but an act of service. Pain, suffering and trauma are passed on through generations until someone in a family is courageous enough to sit through them without judgement, feel them heal, and transform them. It is for the same reason that in the Indian scriptures, those who are on the path of transformation are called 'Dheera', the hero who is full of bravery, strength, and patience.

I arrived at another insight during the same meditation session—that of the science of the transference of knowledge and healing through entanglement. We were once one with our mother; biologically we are entangled with her, though now we seem to be separate in different bodies. We are continuations of our parents. The science of quantum entanglement demonstrates this—when two particles are entangled, they remain connected even light years apart. Despite their vast separation, a change induced in one will affect the other. Similarly, learning and healing are transferred from us to our ancestors. The Indian scriptures mention that if one person attains enlightenment in the family, the fourteen generations of past, present and future are liberated as well.

How can we heal ourselves and our ancestors? The way to do this is to recognize and embody the truth that we are pure Awareness, quite apart from the physical body and the mind with all its conditioning and traumas. As Awareness, we are the subject in which pain arises as an object. It's crucial that we take note of it. If we can see something, it is an object of our perception and therefore separate from us. We must remember that we are the Primordial Seer, existing apart from anything that we see. Let us not allow ourselves to be dragged down by the seen, which is merely an object of our perception. It may be helpful to recognize the pain as an object and clearly label it as such during the process. We should be like tigers, fierce and unafraid in the face of our fears. Running away from them only invites them to haunt us more. Instead, let us immerse ourselves in the present moment. Let any amount of pain or fear flow through us like a passing storm. We should remember that these storms cannot move us an inch, for we are rooted in our presence. I myself have been on a three-month solitary retreat, cutting myself off from the distractions of the world and facing my pain and fears head-on. The experience transformed and healed me in ways I could never have imagined. Remember, our fears can only haunt us until we let them. They are like shadows, appearing as ghosts when not seen for what they truly are. Suffering is a disease that we have fed with overthinking. But we don't have to suffer any more if we don't want to. Stop identifying with painful thoughts and reclaim your power. Bring attention to the Awareness that is watching these thoughts that are feeding the pain in our minds. And instead of tilting the attention towards the thoughts, tilt the attention towards your Awareness.

Lisa Miller, a professor at Columbia University and a clinical psychologist who researches spirituality in psychology, beautifully describes in her TED talk that depression is one side of the door, the other side of which is spirituality. In her research, she found that patients with a long history of depression have atrophy in the same regions of the brain where meditators have thick healthy growth. This suggests that spirituality is an antidote to suffering and sometimes pain is the door to spirituality.

According to the wise Buddhist monk Ajanh Brahm, 'Pain is natural but suffering is optional'. This profound statement underscores the fact that experiencing pain is an inevitable part of life, but allowing it to control us and cause prolonged suffering is a choice we make. Consider the scenario of a newborn—a being free from all kinds of conditioning. Would the death of a sibling or relative affect a newborn? No, because the newborn has yet to establish connection with the deceased and has not yet formed an identity. Can we, then, generate within ourselves the mind of a newborn, free from conditioning, preconceptions and attachments? From our earliest moments, we begin absorbing the beliefs and values of those around us, from our family members to society at large. This early conditioning shapes our understanding of the world and our place in it, often leading us to adopt roles such as mothers, fathers, sisters, brothers, husbands or wives. As we continue to grow, we adopt new ideas and ideologies, aligning ourselves with political movements like communism, leftism or rightism, among others. However, this accumulation of beliefs and conditioning can restrict us, borrowing our essence and fragmenting our sense of self. These ideas come to life within our thoughts and beliefs, and the more we invest in them, the more power and influence they hold over us. Consequently, the more we cling to our pain and rationalize its causes, the more significant and powerful it becomes.

In our journey of healing, let us embrace our true Awareness, acknowledging the pain and fears that arise while maintaining a stance of detached observation. Let us transcend the limitations of conditioned existence, reclaiming our power to shape our own reality. By doing so, we not only heal ourselves but also contribute to the healing of our ancestral lineage, breaking free from the cycles of suffering and opening the door to profound spiritual growth and liberation.

Practical Ideas

The idea that pain can lead to learning and growth is based on the concept of 'post-traumatic growth', which refers to positive changes that can result from experiencing a traumatic event, such as increased resilience, personal strength and a greater appreciation for life. One study published in the *Journal of Consulting and Clinical Psychology* in 2006 found that individuals who reported experiencing post-traumatic growth also reported greater openness to new experiences and a greater sense of personal growth compared to those who did not report post-traumatic growth. Another study published in the journal, *Personality and Social Psychology Review* in 2004, found that people who experienced adversity often developed a new perspective on life that allowed them to find meaning and purpose in their suffering, leading to personal growth.

Furthermore, research on neuroplasticity suggests that the brain is capable of changing and adapting in response to experiences, including pain. The brain can reorganize itself to form new neural connections and pathways, which can lead to learning and growth.

Thich Nhat Hanh wrote in his book *No Mud, No Lotus: The Art of Transforming Suffering*: 'The ground of suffering is also the ground of transformation. If you are able to embrace your suffering and look deeply into it, you can transform it into compassion, understanding and love. This is the miracle of mindfulness. This is the miracle of transformation.' On these lines, I suggest some practical ideas to embrace your suffering and dive right into transformation.

Here are some of the techniques that have helped me in my journey of healing.

Positive self-talk in the face of a stressful event helps me cope well and shields me from anxiety or panic attacks. This ties in with the idea of a growth mindset as I reflect on what I can learn from the situation and how I can improve myself.

Applying these tools prevents me from storing these stressful events as trauma in my body.

Another method that has worked for me is *Vipassana*. Taught by the late S.N. Goenka, the practice is conducted in a strictly regimented way in two-day, three-day and ten-day retreats. To participate in the shorter retreats, completion of a full ten-day retreat is required. I have attended all the formats, starting with the ten-day retreat, which I attended when I was pregnant with my son Nirvanh, unbeknownst to me. Perhaps it was meant for Nirvanh (whose name signifies liberation or eternal bliss) to share that first experience with me. The retreat centre is situated in the scenic and isolated town of Kelseyville in Northern California. The centre's set-up is stunning, with beautiful surroundings.

Upon arrival, you must surrender all forms of stimuli, including cell phones, books, laptops and even pens and notepads. For ten days, you are not allowed to communicate with anyone or make eye contact with others. You cannot write anything down or talk to yourself out loud. Old students are provided with food twice a day, with the last meal served at 11.30 a.m., but tea and coffee are available in the evening. Additionally, you must follow the Buddhist code of ethics known as the five precepts, which prohibits killing of any living beings, stealing, sexual misconduct, lying and the use of intoxicants.

Participating in a Vipassana retreat requires a significant commitment to meditate for hours on end using this specific technique. Guided meditations are played in the voice of S.N. Goenka, the late teacher who brought this practice to the world. The initial days of the retreat are dedicated to developing concentration by focusing on the breath, known as *Anapana* meditation. Once the basic breathing techniques are established, participants proceed to Vipassana meditation, where they sit for hours scanning their entire body for rising sensations. The technique involves acknowledging the sensations without reacting to them, and avoiding indulging in any thoughts that may arise. Stored trauma, known as *samskara* in Sanskrit or *sankhara* in Pali, can also come to the surface during this practice. Whether it is the American psychiatrist Bessel van der Kolk's concept of the body keeping score, the idea of stored trauma I introduced in this book, or Vipassana's sankhara or the Vedantic samskara—the concept is the same. During my first Vipassana retreat, I vividly experienced the sensation of my thighs being slowly axed, which was quite uncomfortable. Another participant even had a seizure during the process, emphasizing the importance of reflecting carefully before signing up for this intense journey.

On one of my days there, we had a scorpion grace us with its venomous presence. Surprisingly, instead of trying to kill it, the participants handled the situation gracefully and released it back into the jungle. This demonstrated our commitment to practising the five precepts. The programme ended with a session on *Metta*, which is all about cultivating loving kindness. Once the programme ended, we were finally allowed to talk to the other participants for the first time. It was a surreal experience to break the silence and connect with others after days of meditative solitude.

While I was at the retreat, my mind became clearer and more focused as I diligently practised the meditations. Upon returning to my room after the retreat, my mind was struck by a brilliant idea. In that peaceful and reflective space, I conceptualized the concept for my meditation and mindfulness-based curriculum for children, which I later named *Damara Kids*.

That was not the only positive outcome of that experience. In fact, plenty of research has been done on Vipassana and a lot of positive outcomes have been ascribed to the practice. One study conducted in the city of Muscat suggests that the practice of Vipassana may help mitigate psychological and psychosomatic distress.[*] Vipassana has also been shown to improve emotional processing. In one study, those who practised Vipassana had lower levels of reactivity compared to the control group.[†] This meditation technique has also been found to increase a sense of overall wellness and self-compassion. Another study shows that Vipassana practitioners have lower levels of stress and are more mindful. Finally, the memory organization that happens during sleep also happens during the practice of Vipassana.

My recommendation is that before you make the leap for the ten-day retreat, slowly transition into a lifestyle that will

---

[*] Manchanda, S., and Tripathi, S. M. (2017). Vipassana meditation: A naturalistic, preliminary observation in Muscat. *Journal of Religion and Health*, 56(1), 1–14.

[†] Cahn, B. R., Delorme, A., and Polich, J. (2013). Enhanced response inhibition and reduced midfrontal theta activity in experienced Vipassana meditators. *NeuroImage*, 71, 48–56.

In this study, the authors investigated the neural correlates of response inhibition among experienced Vipassana meditators using EEG (electroencephalography) recordings. The study found that the meditators exhibited enhanced response inhibition compared to a control group, as well as reduced midfrontal theta activity, which is thought to reflect attentional processes.

be more conducive to starting this programme. If you have a lot of Stored Trauma and have been distracting yourself from it by living a hyperstimulated life, you might not be able to deal with this sudden cut-off from stimulation. Talk to your therapist to figure out if it is safe for you to take on this experience.

Finally, a rather impractical yet essential method that has worked for me in my healing is solitary retreats. I do them for one month at a stretch. I have taken three such trips at the time of writing this chapter. I started taking these trips after Sushant's death. I went for the first time around his first death anniversary in June 2021. I was disconnected from the entire world, including my family for the entire month of June.

The spot I go to is in the mountains of California, near a town called Ragged Point. It's a Buddhist institution called Land of Calm Abiding (LOCA) and I had to put in an application to be selected for it. The first time around, they denied my application. I wrote again, providing my credentials of having attended Vipassana retreats in the past, the sincerity of my spiritual seeking, and references from my spiritual teachers. Only then did they budge and let me in.

Your family or friend needs to drop you to Ragged Point and pick you up from the same location at a predetermined date and time. A caretaker comes to Ragged Point to pick you up—only 4x4 trucks and all terrain vehicles can reach all the way to the secluded cabins of meditators.

There is no human interaction other than some written note exchanges with the caretaker for the entire month. There is no cell phone network or internet in the region. You get a small cabin with a kitchen and refrigerator. I brought groceries for the entire month at once. There is an option to bring groceries for two weeks at the end of which you can write a note to the caretaker for the items you want, and the caretaker can go to town and get them for you. The caretaker goes into town once every two weeks and it takes them two hours just to drive back and forth to the store. No money exchanges hands while you are at the retreat because money supposedly distracts us from the practice. If you avail of the grocery service, you either pay upfront before your retreat starts or pay at the end of the month once you are ready to leave.

To let the caretaker know that you are not dead, you need to bring out a red flag, on Mondays and Thursdays, to the front of the cabin. The caretaker makes note of the flag from a distance and does not bother you for the entire month as long as the flag keeps coming out twice a week.

I have had a lot of spiritual experiences and received a lot of wisdom and insight at the cabin. I will go into those details soon in this book. I recommend this practice to anyone who is ready to face pain head-on. Whether it is the pain of losing a loved one or some other pain you are dealing with, such month-long solitary retreats can transform your pain into a catalyst for growth and development.* There are many such practices the details of which I will cover over the course of this book.

---

* However, such long durations of solitude require some preparation and are not meant for everyone. You should always consult your mental health care provider before taking on a challenge of this magnitude.

2

Recognizing the Problem

'If reality did not exist, could there be any knowledge of existence?'—Ramana Maharshi

In the previous chapter, we dissected pain thoroughly. We understood its sources, from childhood trauma to grief in adulthood. We touched upon the idea that pain is inevitable but suffering is optional. In this chapter, we will try to figure out why we suffer if it's optional. Once we recognize the problem (the cause of our suffering), only then will we be able to solve it.

The question might arise—*Isn't my own existence the root of all my problems?* A promising answer to this would then be—*This limited being that I feel I am, is the problem. If only I can get rid of this limited 'I', the individual self that I feel I am, I will be happier.*

The pain and dissatisfaction caused by this limited 'I', the egoic identity, run deep and have accumulated momentum because of the universal acceptance of this being normal. We will never be happy as long as we think we are finite and limited because our real nature is infinite and unlimited. It's only for a while that we can fool ourselves into believing that if only this particular problem gets resolved or that desire gets fulfilled, will we be happy. But the eternal happiness that the mind promises through the riddance of a problem or by the fulfilment of a desire, if properly explored, is elusive, to say the least. Tomorrow, some other problem will arise in its place. Some other desire will occupy the mind and again we will become restless and suffer.

So, is there a way out of this incessant suffering?

Yes, there is a way out. The cause of all pain and suffering is the identification with the false sense of 'I' and the way out is to engage in the investigation of the real nature of 'I'.

Who Am I? It is the question we all start with and to answer the question, we work hard to make something or someone of ourselves. But we generally tend to forget that the more we work towards solidifying our identity as this individual self, the further we move away from the reality of our infinite Self. The more we define ourselves, the more we confine ourselves. We feel suffocated because we are trying to limit that infinite within the boundaries of this individual self. The sense of separateness we hold on to is the cause of all our anxieties and depressions, all our sufferings. We can never feel whole by being an isolated island.

From childhood, we are fed the idea that we must make something of ourselves; we must chase success, money, power and fame, and only once we have achieved them are we truly worthy. So we blindly get into this rat race, incessantly pursuing these goals for ego-gratification. In this process, the mind, as a tool, starts to serve the egoic or lower self in us. Everything that is done is laden with self-motive. We see other people as means to the goal of our egoic gratification.

What is it that makes us feel separate from others and our surroundings?

The ego is nothing but a set of beliefs, ideas, early childhood conditioning, memories and our unquestioned conviction that we are nothing apart from this body-mind complex. It is what makes us feel separate from others and our surroundings. The egoic identification with the body-mind construct only leads to suffering. This egoic self is inherently limited and lacks wholeness. Desires are the offshoot of such lack. Because we feel limited, we try to fill ourselves with the fulfilment of desires, such as the desire for money, power, prestige, success, worldly knowledge, a special relationship and so on. But the fulfilment of any personal desire satiates the egoic mind only for the time being, then it rises again with more fervour, deeper cravings and more and more desires. It drives a constant struggle that there is no end to as we look for satisfaction in externalities. It's an insatiable mad quest, a compulsive pursuit for ego-gratification to feel fulfilled.

Two things can happen in this pursuit of happiness and fulfilment. Either our desires get met and we soon realize their inadequacy to keep us eternally satiated, or they are not fulfilled and we feel a sense of anger and resentment. The truth is that the ego's needs can never be met because the ego that we are trying to feed is a hallucination, an imposter self. It is not there in reality; it merely appears to exist. The problem is our identification with the egoic self.

What is the egoic self composed of?

Body identification, mind identification and identification with the character or role we are playing in life make up the egoic self. We are the one unchanging Awareness, but it's hard to see this truth when we are so entrenched in our egoic selves. We will explore more about the egoic self later in the chapter.

Misidentification with the Physical Body

Our identification with the physical body runs deep and is integral to our being. We think we end at the folds of our skin. It is common for people to identify closely with their physical bodies and to view their bodies as an integral part of their identities. This type of identification is known as 'Embodiment'.

The body, a tool for perception, is considered to be our self, our reality. Why? Because we experience the world of perception through this body. But we don't consider the world as ourselves, then why this particular body? The sense of aliveness that is felt integral to the body is considered as 'I' and the body is considered as 'mine'. But at times, we say, 'this is my body' and at other times, we say, 'I am the body'. How do we make such a big error? Something that belongs to us, how can it be us? Do we ever say that I am my house? No, for that would be insane! But we do say that I am the body. Why? Because when our body is touched, *we* feel touched, when our body is in pain, *we* feel the pain. The pleasure and pain sensations experienced by the body become our experience and therefore we feel we are the body.

However, it is important to recognize and remember that the body is simply a vessel that allows us to experience the world around us and that our true identity extends beyond the physical form. The gross physical body is a tool for perception and a conglomeration of different sensations. Let's dive deep to see how we are not our physical bodies.

Consider these five reasons to set us apart from the assumption that we are the gross experienced body:

1. **Observer and the Observed:** We are the observer and the body is the observed. The sensations of pain and pleasure in the body can be observed and we, as Awareness, are above the experience of the pain and pleasure of the body.

   The observer can never be the observed. Let me explain this further. The physical body, as we know it, is composed of the five senses of sight, hearing, taste, smell and touch. These five senses help us in experiencing the world of pain and pleasure around us. If we look closely enough, we realize that this physical body is not only composed of senses but is, in itself, a conglomeration of different sensations. Vipassana is a wonderful practice to observe this. It is important to recognize that the Self, or the sense of being, exists independently of the body and its experiences. The Self is the subjective experience of consciousness; it is the sense of 'I Am' that experiences the world through the body and its senses.

In this sense, it could be said that the Self is above the experience of pain and pleasure in the body, as it is the Self that is aware of and interprets these experiences. It is the Self that notices the body's experiences, rather than the other way around.

2. **Unchanging Awareness and the Changing Body:** We are the unchanging Awareness, while the body is continuously changing. The body goes through several changes, from a child's body to a teenage body to an adult body to an old and ageing body, but we feel the same 'I' inside the body. We have a sense of continuity and sameness over time, remaining the same 'I' throughout the various stages of life, even as the body changes. This sense of continuity and sameness is often referred to as a 'sense of self' or 'self-concept'. I am in no way trying to imply that our 'self-concept' is the real 'I' or who we are. But self-concept is the way that we perceive ourselves; it is the imposter self that we will cover later in another chapter. It includes our thoughts, beliefs and feelings about who we are and what we are like. It is shaped by our experiences, our relationships and our cultural and social context. Even though our physical body undergoes many changes throughout life, the self-concept often remains relatively stable and consistent.

Moreover, the sensations of pain and pleasure in the body are also continuously changing. They rise and fall, come and go. We cannot hold on to the pleasures of the body or run away from its pain. How can we be the changing bodily sensations, when we know ourselves to be the unchanging witness to them? It is a common experience to feel that the self, or the sense of 'I', is a constant presence whereas the sensations and experiences of the body are changing. We are the unchanging Awareness and not the changing sensations of the body.

3. **Permanent Awareness and the Impermanent Body:** Where is the physical body during deep sleep? We don't experience the physical body during deep sleep. But how can we be the non-existent physical body during deep sleep when we know ourselves to be ever existing?

We don't experience our own physical body during deep sleep as our senses are largely inactive and there is no experience of the external world either. However, the Awareness that we are does not disappear during deep sleep. We do get up after a good night's sleep and exclaim 'I slept like a log!' Who was the one aware of this sleep? We are separate from our physical body as we can exist in the absence of it; the Awareness that 'we are' is not lost or reduced during deep sleep.

During deep sleep, we experience pure darkness or blankness. The Awareness has nothing to be aware of or, in better terms, the Awareness is aware of the darkness of deep sleep. That's why when we get up in the morning there is a recollection of deep or disturbed sleep. Indeed, we feel completely rejuvenated after a good night's sleep.

It is because all the limitations of body and mind have been lifted for a while. During deep sleep, everything that we are not is dropped—identification with the body, the mind and the character. The burden of being a certain someone is dropped, and all limitations are stripped off and we take a dip in the infinite ocean of our true Being. Infinitude is our real nature. That's why when we define ourselves in terms of our body and mind, we feel a sense of confinement.

A physical body might be in pain or be diseased but when we are in deep sleep, we do not experience any pain in the body. This experience of not being aware of the physical body or any bodily discomfort during deep sleep can be seen as a temporary glimpse of the true nature of the Self as something that exists beyond the body and its experiences.

4. **Sentient Awareness and the Insentient Body:** We, as Awareness, have sentience—our self-consciousness and the ability to think, feel or experience the world—on our side, which the body does not. The body is a complex system of cells, tissues and organs that performs a wide range of functions, but it does not have the capacity of being aware of itself or having a subjective experience. Just as the moon doesn't have any light of its own but borrows the light of the sun, the body borrows its sentience from us, the consciousness. The mind, which includes the brain and the nervous system, interprets the input from the senses and generates thoughts, feelings and experiences. It is the mind that gives us the sense of being a self, or an 'I', that is aware of and experiences the world through the body.

A great thought experiment proposed by Greg Goode allows us to confirm that the body lacks self-consciousness. Raise your hand and say hello to it. Does the hand say 'Hello' back to you? No, it does not and if it were to, it would scare us out of our wits. Why? Because the body does not have the capacity for self-awareness or subjective experience. It is not capable of independent thought or action.

Another experiment is the 'rubber hand illusion', a psychological phenomenon that involves the manipulation of sensory input to create the impression that an artificial hand is part of an individual's own body. This illusion is often used in scientific studies to investigate how the brain processes and integrates information from different senses and how it constructs a sense of body ownership.

In the 'rubber hand illusion', the subject individual sits at a table with their arm hidden from view and an artificial hand placed in front of them. The individual then watches as the experimenter strokes both the individual's real hand (which is hidden) and the artificial hand in sync. After a few minutes, many subjects begin to feel as if the artificial hand is part of their own body, with some even reporting feeling as if they are looking at their own hand when they see the artificial hand being touched.

This illusion reveals that the brain can construct a sense of body ownership based on sensory input. The brain is able to integrate information from different senses (such as touch and vision) to construct a coherent and unified sense of the body. Thus, when an individual experiences the rubber hand illusion, they may feel as if the artificial hand is part of their own body, even though it is physically separate. This suggests that the sense of body ownership and the sense of self are not necessarily tied to the physical body itself, but rather are constructed by the brain based on sensory input. It illustrates how we start identifying ourselves with the gross physical body through unreliable sensory inputs.

5. **One and Many:** Awareness is always experienced as One. The body, on the other hand, has many parts—legs, hands, head and so on. The sense of unity and oneness that we experience in our physical body is a result of the way the brain processes and integrates information from the various parts of the body. Our brain receives input from all the different senses and systems in the body and integrates this information to construct a coherent and unified sense of the body.

   This sense of a mental representation of the body that allows us to move and interact with the world in a coordinated and purposeful way is known as the 'body schema'. The concept includes not only the physical layout of the body and its parts but also the sensory and motor information that is associated with each part. As a result of this integration, we experience a sense of unity and oneness with the various parts of our physical body, and we feel as if we are a single, cohesive entity. So, what we consider as 'I', the body, is merely the mental representation of the body in the mind that helps us navigate the multiplicity of the body.

   We can consider several other compelling factors to understand and establish ourselves as separate from the body identity. For example, when we are under the influence of anaesthesia, we are hardly aware of any bodily sensations, including pain. This too can be used as a piece of evidence that the Self is separate from the body. In a state of flow or samadhi, again, we are hardly aware of our physical body. Whenever we are completely consumed by the work we are doing, in a state of flow, we don't experience the heaviness of the gross body. Similarly, in the state of samadhi when our whole focus is absorbed in a single point, we completely disconnect from experiencing our body.

There have been compelling pieces of evidence that we are separate from our physical bodies in people's accounts of NDEs. People who have been deemed clinically dead with no measurable brain function or heart rate have come back to life and have reported experiencing the surroundings and events so precisely while they were clinically dead that they can't be scientifically brushed aside. Anita Moorjani, whose story I shared earlier, has had a mind-bending and fascinating NDE experience. In her book, she beautifully describes her disconnection from her physical body while she was admitted to the hospital. She vividly illustrates how she felt herself leaving her physical body and experiencing a sense of peace and understanding that she had never felt before. She felt no emotional connection to her physical body as she drifted away into the embrace of infinite, unconditional love. Though she wasn't using her five biological senses, she was acutely aware of her surroundings as if by the sheer power of her consciousness.

Moorjani's near-death experience is not uncommon, and many people who have had NDEs have reported feeling a sense of separation from their physical body and a sense of transcendence or enlightenment. How can they experience their surroundings even though their physical bodies are lying seemingly unconscious on the hospital bed? Are we more than our physical bodies? These are a few questions we can ponder.

I present these arguments so that we can disconnect from the identification with our physical body. The realization that we are not merely our limited physical body can be a truly transformative experience and can have several benefits. Recognizing that our sense of self is not confined to our physical body can invoke a true sense of liberation, freedom and inner peace. We develop greater self-awareness and a deeper understanding of our thoughts, feelings and experiences.

Seeing ourselves as something beyond our physical body can help us gain a greater sense of perspective and help us to see the world differently. This understanding can help us in reaching a greater sense of connectedness with others and the world around us because the demarcation of the physical body has been erased. Seeing ourselves as something beyond our physical body can help us to cultivate a greater sense of inner peace, as we recognize that our sense of self is not tied to our physical body and the pursuits of adorning the body and seeking to overly pamper the body are in vain. We can do what is necessary to keep the body healthy by neither starving it to death nor feeding it till we fall ill and avoiding any kind of extremes of self-indulgence and self-denial—balance is the key.

I would like to share one of my personal stories here. When I had gone for the Vipassana retreat, during one of my seatings, I felt a deep clamouring pain around my upper thigh, as if an axe were cutting through it. We were instructed not to move or react during the rise of any sensation, however painful or pleasant. So, I couldn't continue to move my attention to every part of my body. The pain was so excruciating that it kept seeking my attention. But I stuck to the Vipassana technique and continued with the practice. After close to fifteen minutes, the pain had reduced considerably, becoming close to nil.

When I was feeling the pain, it seemed as if nothing else mattered. Nothing else came to my mind at that time, it drew all my attention. But following the exact instructions of Vipassana and not moving or in any way reacting to the impulse or the sensations made me realize that everything is temporary, no matter how intense it might feel at the moment. Everything does subside with time. What we need to have is patience and faith in the teachings. One thing that has always worked for me is that I have childlike faith and deep, penetrating intensity.

I will take this opportunity to explain a bit more about the Vipassana technique. Vipassana meditation is a practice based on the teachings of the Buddha. It originated in ancient India and is now practised in many parts of the world. The word 'vipassana' literally means 'to see things as they really are', and the practice is intended to help practitioners to cultivate insight and wisdom. In Vipassana meditation, practitioners focus their attention on the present moment and their own experience, without judgement or interpretation. This involves paying attention to the breath, the body and the sensations arising and falling in the body. One needs to observe them with a sense of openness and curiosity.

The goal of Vipassana meditation is to cultivate a sense of clarity and understanding about the nature of the mind and the world, and to develop qualities such as equanimity, compassion and mindfulness. Many people benefit from Vipassana meditation. It has not only been proven to reduce stress but to also promote a sense of well-being and inner peace.

There is a growing body of scientific research on the potential benefits of Vipassana meditation, which suggests that the practice may have several positive effects on physical and mental health. Some of the potential benefits of practising Vipassana meditation, in addition to promoting a sense of overall well-being and inner peace, are listed below:

- Reducing stress and anxiety: Research has suggested that Vipassana meditation may be effective in reducing stress and anxiety, as well as in improving coping skills and boosting resilience.
- Improving sleep: Vipassana meditation may help to improve sleep quality and reduce sleep problems, such as insomnia.
- Reducing pain: Some research has found that Vipassana meditation may be effective in reducing chronic pain and improving the ability to cope with pain.
- Improving cardiovascular health: Vipassana meditation may have a positive impact on cardiovascular health, including reducing blood pressure and improving heart rate variability.

- Enhancing cognitive function: This meditation may improve cognitive function, such as attention and memory, and may also have a positive impact on brain structure and function.

- Overcoming Addiction: Vipassana meditation can help manage addiction and reduce the urge to engage in addictive behaviours. Vipassana meditation helps in promoting mindfulness, which is the ability to be fully present and aware in the moment. This, in turn, helps overcome addiction. By cultivating mindfulness through this meditation, individuals may be better able to recognize and manage their cravings and make healthier choices. By reducing stress and improving coping skills, this meditation technique helps individuals to better manage the challenges and stressors that contribute to addiction.

These are merely the corollary benefits of practising Vipassana; the main purpose of the technique is to attain spiritual insights which help us experience our inherent bliss and wholeness. During Vipassana meditation, we experience our bodies in the form of sensations. We notice that we are averse to certain sensations and drawn to some others, a play of attraction and aversion, called '*raag*' and '*dwesh*' respectively, in Sanskrit. We can note the same kind of attraction or aversion towards worldly objects. When we experience a bodily sensation or encounter a worldly object that we find pleasurable, we feel a sense of liking or attraction towards it. On the other hand, if we experience a bodily sensation or encounter a worldly object that we find unpleasant, we may feel a sense of dislike or aversion towards it. These feelings can be the result of past experiences, cultural and social conditioning and individual preferences. But at the primal level, most human beings are averse to pain and crave pleasure. We are inherently wired to chase things that please us and avoid things or situations that produce pain or discomfort.

Is there a way we can overcome our primal instinct of being pulled and pushed by our cravings and aversions?

Practising Vipassana and becoming aware of the present moment helps us in cultivating a sense of equanimity or detachment from our likes and dislikes. Through the power of these practices, we recognize and become witnesses to our likes and dislikes, cravings and aversions. This mindfulness creates a certain amount of space between us and the likes and dislikes we notice in our minds. This distance allows us to see that none of our likes and dislikes are permanent or absolute, which gives us more control over our reactions and behaviour. We are not blindly pulled or pushed according to our cravings and aversions. There is a sense of equanimity that dawns, which produces detachment, greater inner peace and clarity in us. We feel grounded and centred in our true nature of unadulterated Awareness.

The Body Is Nothing but a Food Sheath

The *Taittiriya Upanishad*, a Hindu text, states that our body is nothing but a food sheath (*annamaya kosha*). It is sustained by what we drink and eat and is ultimately the source of all material existence. The *Upanishad* says that the body should be cared for and respected, as it is the temple of the soul.

Here is a beautiful experiment. Take an apple, call it an apple when you are holding it in your hand and now eat it. Where has the apple gone? It is part of your body now and you have immediately started calling it 'my body'. When it was outside you and had a form, you called it an apple, and now it is no more an apple; it is you! So why did we start calling an apple 'our body'? And not only 'our body' but 'Me', because we consider this body as 'I'. The physical body is sustained by the food we eat, and this food becomes part of our body once it is consumed. This process of the food becoming part of our body is a metaphor for how the material world becomes a part of us, and of our physical body being a reflection of the material world. When we don't consider the world as 'I', why do we consider the physical body as 'I'?

After understanding the misidentification with the body and its contribution to the egoic self, let's now investigate the misidentification with the mind.

Misidentification with the Mind

The mind is our power of imagination; thoughts get produced by this process of imagination. Craving and aversion are the basic foundations of the mind and all thoughts arise from them.

To elaborate, our identification with the physical body gives rise to thoughts of survival. Whatever helps the body survive is considered favourable, therefore resulting in pleasant sensations in the body. The mind, in turn, gets encoded with the pleasurable sensations of the body and craves more of them in the form of desires. Whatever threatens the body's survival is considered unfavourable and therefore results in unpleasant sensations in the body; the mind gets encoded with the unpleasant sensations of the body and develops an aversion towards them in the form of fear.

Labels, concepts, ideas, words and judgements are all produced by this mind, creating a screen of separation between you and others. This separateness solidifies the ego identity further. Now we are not only our physical bodies but we have also become this set of beliefs we are invested in. We form all sorts of identifications and keep limiting ourselves further and further.

Ramana Maharshi beautifully defined the mind as a bundle of thoughts. Every moment, he said, the mind rises as a single thought. Memories from the past and imaginations of the future rise as a thought in the present. What Ramana means here is that the mind is not a separate identity we need to fight. If we start believing the mind to be a separate identity, we have to fight and defeat it to find our real selves. That way we will never find it because it has no separate existence apart from the thought that is rising in the present moment. And we are always equipped to handle a single thought in the present moment with Awareness.

Recognizing the problem is half the battle won. When we seek fulfilment through the mind, we fall prey to greed, pride and self-limiting beliefs, and then we suffer because they are not our true nature. This, then, marks the beginning of *samsara*.

What is Samsara? And is there a way out of samsara?

Samsara is believing that we are the limited body-mind entity and nothing beyond that, and then acting in accordance with the mind-created self. This mind-created self has many limiting beliefs which let desires and fear enter our psyche. As Buddha rightly said, 'Desire is the cause of all suffering'; we suffer because we bind ourselves with numberless desires. The fulfilment of these desires leads to more desires and their non-fulfilment leads to pain, anger and grievances. These desires run so deep in our psyche that it feels nearly impossible to get rid of them. All we need is basic food, clothing and shelter to maintain our physical body; healthy nurturing relationships for our emotional body (the heart); and good education for the development of our mental body (the mind/intellect). Other than these, all desires are acquired. When we incessantly feed our desires and pursue them, we find ourselves burnt out in the process.

Here is a story of two brothers: They were born into a relatively well-to-do family. They had enough to eat and drink, a good house to live in and an opportunity to acquire good education and values. They even enjoyed the love of their family and friends. As they grew up, they got married and had their own families. The elder brother started following a spiritual and balanced lifestyle. He not only worked and provided for his family, but even found time for his spiritual practices like reading spiritual books and practising yoga and meditation. He had started living a wholesome life. He made regular donations, did charity and, in whatever capacity he could, served his community, as a result of which he generated a lot of *punya* (merits). And the merit generated by him not only helped him live a fulfilling life but helped his family members too. He became a blessing not only to his family but also to the entire community at large.

On the other hand, the younger brother who was considered very bright and intelligent did well financially but eventually became greedy and a miser and started to hoard money for his future. He wanted to make enough money so that he wouldn't have to work in the future. In the process, he became too focused on money and the benefits he thought money would bring in the future. He taught the same to his children. He stopped sharing his wealth and giving to the needy. He became more and more self-centred. He developed all kinds of vices, he started taking drugs, drank alcohol, ate meat, and tried to cheat on taxes to save more money. He even made his wife's life miserable. He took all her money and hoarded it too, making it completely impossible for her to help any poor or needy. He had become completely obsessive about money and spoilt all his relationships with people because of that. Eventually, he started to have poor mental health, due to which he lost his job. He also lost all the money that he had saved for his future in one of the market crashes. Nobody came to help him in his time of need, and because of the values he had taught his children, even they had become self-centred like him. He created a miserable life for himself and for the people around him.

This story shows how desires can create further desires and lead us deeper into suffering. It also shows that there is a way out of this suffering or samsara. And the way out is knowledge about our own real Self. Self-knowledge can be reached through investigation and clear observation.

Let's perform an experiment to better understand how samsara works. Imagine a newborn's mind. When a child is born, her mind is like an open sky. She doesn't have any preconceived notions or any sort of identification. Her mind is pure like the sky. Now imagine that the sky is filled with stars, considering the stars to be the images the child is exposed to, like different people, things and places over time. They all appear in the mind of the child and there is no conflict. The problem starts when instead of focusing on the whole expanse of the sky with the stars and everything, we fragment the sky by naming the celestial bodies.

Doing so is almost like constricting the child to be focused on a single star and not the whole sky. Similarly, when we give a name to a child and teach her that this particular body is her body, she feels isolated from all the other bodies and develops a mind and ego. The child has now become one star, alienated from all the other stars and the openness of the sky. When that star sees a bigger, brighter star, it feels inferior and when that star sees other smaller and dimmer stars, it feels a sense of pride. The openness of the sky full of stars is still available but the focus has been placed on only one single star. The trick is to simply shift the focus from one single star to the expanse of the sky.

In the same way, to be free of samsara, we need to shift our focus from one single mind and be synonymous with the ever-present witness consciousness in us. What do we need to do for that? It is important to note that Awareness can never be negated. Try to not be aware for a moment—it is impossible! We are helplessly aware. We are even aware of the darkness or blankness of deep sleep. That which is not there in deep sleep is an illusion. The lower self or the knower of the world is not present during deep sleep, hence, it is false.

Then who is the knower Self and what is this world of perception?

The knower Self, when looked at closely, collapses into the real Self. For example, when a rope that is mistaken to be a snake in the dark is given a closer look, it is found to be nothing else other than a rope. The world of perception too, when seen through the eyes of knowledge, is nothing but the real Self, appearing as the observed universe of name and form. The awakened ones know that there is no world separate from themselves. Knowledge, when filtered through the mind, shines as an understanding of the world around us. Mental functioning is illumined and made possible by the background of Awareness. Ignorance, which is deemed to be the cause of the phenomenal world, seems to take flight with the dawn of knowledge. Where there is light, there is no space for darkness.

Why do we think we are the mind?

Because we don't know that we are the Self, the luminary of the mind.

Then what is the mind?

Mind is the power of imagination of the Self. It is not apart from the Self. When the Self seeks to find or experience itself, the mind is born of the divine womb, thoughts are generated and the world of perception is created. Thought is the nature of the mind. Whenever there is no thought, there is no mind and hence, no world. Therefore, there is no world during deep sleep because of the absence of the mind. When the mind is completely quiet with no trace of thought, that is when the mind is completely pure. And in the pure mind, only Awareness shines forth.

The mind comprises four components:

- **Thinking mind:** the continuous series of thoughts
- **Intellect:** the power of understanding or discernment, which tells us right from wrong
- **Memories:** the stored impressions of the individual self
- **Ego:** the role/character we think we are

Three reasons why we are not our minds:

The reasons for not being the mind are similar to those for not being the physical body. We, as Awareness, are one, unchanging and permanent, but the thoughts in our minds are relatively many, changing and temporary.

- We are prior to the thoughts in our minds. Why? Because we can observe them. They are an object to our ever-present witnessing Self.

- Thoughts rise and fall; they have a temporary existence. We, as pure consciousness, are ever-existent. How can we be something that comes and goes? There is no existence of thoughts during deep sleep.

- Thoughts are many and keep changing. We, as pure consciousness, are one and the constant unchanging witness of the ever-changing mind.

Why do we identify so deeply with the thoughts in our minds and why do we feel the need to act on them?

Ignorance leads us to identify with our thoughts. We have not taken the time to take a closer look at who we are in reality and instead are instinctively pulled and pushed by our thoughts. We operate in the world by a set of assumptions that we quietly accept because this set of unquestioned assumptions is running everybody and the world around us. Questioning them would mean being an outcast, somebody who cannot follow the set rules, or a maverick.

But if we are sensitive enough, life wakes us up and we start questioning the universally acceptable assumptions. We, as the waking lot, cannot live like herds any more or follow the rat race and the herd mentality. We are not ready to be hypnotized by the media and the floating worldly talks and news. There can be many causes of this awakening—a close experience with death or the death of a loved one or excruciating suffering or disease.

As we start waking up and understanding the knowledge that we are pure Awareness, above the body and mind, the identification with the mind begins to weaken. We have more control over our thoughts and decisions, and understand which thoughts are necessary to act upon.

We are wired to respond to our thoughts and feelings as if they are real because this has been helping us survive in the past. The feeling of fear prompted the early humans to run away from dangerous situations, while the feeling of hunger prompted them to find food. So our thoughts and feelings served as signals to act. But, in today's day and age, thinking has become compulsive. Most of us are obsessed with our thinking. There is no space between our thoughts and us.

Many thoughts are imagined. For example, our mind can imagine that somebody is trying to hurt us even when there is no truth in that. We start looking at the world around us with suspicion, as if in survival mode. We judge people, try to create unnecessary boundaries, lose trust and create more misery for ourselves in the process. Such thought processes and the feelings associated with them can become very problematic when they are too intense or persistent and are not based on reality.

Painful incidents generally colour our perspective towards life in a gloomy shade. Though things and situations might be completely alright on the outside, we nonetheless find our mind engaging in finding faults with people and situations around us. I am not saying that there might not be people you have to stay away from for the time being. At times, it is not only advisable but necessary to stay away from certain people and situations. A growing plant is caged so that it can be protected from animals that could eat it up but once the tree is fully grown and blooming, it has no fear of survival.

Similarly, in the beginning, when training our minds and growing our practice, we have to keep away from difficult situations and people, but once our realization has fructified completely, there isn't any need to shelter ourselves from any situation or people, no matter how intense or difficult. You will become like the unwavering, fully grounded tree which can offer shade to others too.

Misidentification with the Character

The egoic self is the root of all problems, the greatest delusion we fall prey to. After the identification with the body and mind happens, the ego is born—or you could say that the birth of the ego gives rise to the identification with the body-mind complex.

What is ego?

The ego is the fourth and innermost component of the mind—the possessor of the body and mind. It also rises as a thinker in us. The mind is like a lens, with the capacity to catch the reflection of the sun, the Awareness that we are. The reflection of the Awareness caught in the mind is the sense of ego and what we consider ourselves to be. Once the egoic self takes possession of our real Self, we get into the pattern of compulsive thinking. The egoic self gives rise to individuality and forms a sense of separateness from the world around us. It has a compulsive need to constantly solidify its own existence by identifying with the thought patterns in the mind. The egoic self feeds the thoughts and the thoughts feed the egoic self. The egoic self is in a constant struggle to survive in this foreign world that it deems separate from it. It even catches hold of the body and claims its existence as its own. This ego-self is always looking to gain something from others and the world. This wanting to gain more and more solidifies the ego further.

When we view the egoic self through the lens of Awareness, it transforms into a beautiful expression of the divine play. In truth, the roles we play in the world are manifestations of the infinite in the finite. Each one of us is an avatar of the Infinite, born out of a state of fullness and bliss. The Vedas feature a mantra that speaks of this concept, highlighting that we have originated from a state of completeness. The mantra acknowledges the inherent wholeness and completeness of the universe and everything within it. It reminds us that even when we take something away from the whole, the whole remains complete and unchanging.

What or who is an avatar?

We are all an avatar. We are all expressions of that infinite, wonderfully and blissfully playing a role. When a role doesn't bind us, we are an avatar; when the role binds us, we become puny egos, caught in a compulsive storyline. The avatar in us is free of a storyline but can play a character in a story impeccably. It can take pauses and stay free of the story when required. The egoic self, on the other hand, has the compulsive urge to play the storyline constantly. It cannot disconnect from the character it is playing at will. It relies on a set of memories to lend it a reality. It tries to ape the ever-present Awareness in us, which it is not. Our thoughts must keep feeding the egoic self with constant thoughts related to the storyline; thus the conception of past and future times takes place.

Memories are created in the present, and that's why memories are so unreliable; they are not simply a record of the past. When we remember something, the brain retrieves information from storage and reassembles it in the present moment. The process of remembering is not a passive process of playing back a recording, but an active process of reconstructing the past based on the information that is currently available in the brain. Scientists, too, have proven memory's inconsistencies. If we closely examine the process of remembering, and delve into the ways the brain stores, processes and retrieves memories, we can figure out how certain memories sometimes prove unreliable. Actually, the whole of memory is unreliable; it is just that we need certain memories to function and continue playing our roles, which is why we believe in them and give them a reality.

What and how much of our memory is actually true?

It is quite difficult to determine if a snippet of memory is true, as memories can be influenced by various factors such as emotions, past experiences and cognitive biases. Research has shown that memories can be distorted or altered over time, which can lead to inaccuracies or inconsistencies. Additionally, the act of retrieving a memory can change the memory itself, potentially making it less reliable. Depending on other people's recollections is unreliable too, as they add their own biases and interpretations.

Neuroimaging techniques such as fMRI (functional magnetic resonance imaging) and PET (positron emission tomography) have provided valuable insights into the neural mechanisms of memory, and have helped to identify the brain regions and processes that are involved in memory formation and retrieval. They have also shown that different types of memory are mediated by different brain regions and that different regions are specialized for different types of information. These techniques have revealed that memories can be influenced by emotions and cognitive biases and that different patterns of brain activity are associated with true and false memories. By understanding the neural processes that underlie memory, scientists are gaining a better understanding of how memories can be unreliable.

One example of a thought experiment that demonstrates the unreliability of memory is the 'Lost in the Mall' technique. This technique was developed by researchers to demonstrate the ease with which false memories can be created. The technique involves asking a person to imagine an event that never occurred, such as getting lost in a shopping mall as a child, and then asking them to recall the imagined event as if it were a real memory. A significant number of people who participate in the experiment develop a detailed and vivid 'memory' of the imagined event, even though it never occurred in reality. This demonstrates that memories can be easily influenced by imagination, expectations and suggestions, and that it is possible to create false memories.

Another example of a thought experiment that illustrates the unreliability of memory is the 'Mandela effect', a phenomenon where a large group of people have the same false memory of an event, historical fact or detail that never occurred. The phenomenon gets its name from a collective false memory that Nelson Mandela died in prison in the 1980s. Many people recall seeing the news of his death and even the funeral on TV, while in reality, he was released in 1990 and died in 2013.

What is the role of memory?

The function of memory is to enable us to play a certain character or role in the world. Memory plays a huge role in forming the egoic self. We form a sense of self by identifying with the roles we play in the world. For example, I, as Shweta, think of myself as a mother, as a wife, as a friend and so on. Then we even add adjectives to these roles we play—I, for instance, am a good and giving mother who has sacrificed a lot for my children. These are added details to the character sketch. We behave as we think we are and we think as we behave, thus forming a vicious circle. Our roles are often based on past experiences and memories, and they shape the way we see ourselves and interact with others. They are mostly inspired by the people whom we have closely observed. So repeating your own mother's patterns will come naturally to you. Breaking subconscious patterns requires higher energy.

We often identify with our thoughts and emotions and see them as a part of ourselves. This can lead to attachment to certain thoughts or emotions, and cause suffering when they change. We also identify with past experiences, especially traumatic ones. This can shape our sense of self and influence our beliefs, values and behaviour. For example, a person who has experienced abuse may see themselves as a victim, and this identification can shape their self-perception and interactions with others.

Memories play a significant role in shaping our sense of self, our beliefs and values, and how we see ourselves and interact with the world. It's important to be aware of the potential limitations of our memories and to be mindful of any potential biases or distortions that may be impacting our perception of ourselves and the world around us.

In truth, we are creating or painting our character at every moment. Our sense of self, or the character we are playing in the world, is constantly being created and shaped in the present moment by our experiences, thoughts, emotions and the level of understanding we are at. It is not a fixed or unchanging entity, but rather a dynamic and ever-changing representation that is influenced by our current state of mind, emotions and experiences. This is why our sense of self can change over time as our experiences and understanding of the world evolve. It's also why it is important to be aware of the potential biases and limitations of our memories and to constantly question and examine our beliefs, values and perceptions of ourselves and the world. The practice of being aware of the character we are playing in the world helps us to see the world as a play. The idea is to become aware of the Self as the observer and not the character, and to detach from the ever-changing roles and characters. Only then can we reach liberation and freedom from suffering.

Creating a positive character sketch for ourselves and following it can be a powerful tool for shaping our sense of self and experiencing a magical and mystical world. When we realize that this world is nothing more than a dream, then the point becomes how to live a purer and better dream where love reigns supreme, where kindness and compassion are our superpowers.

Here are a few steps we can take to create a positive character sketch for ourselves:

Define your values and goals: Start by identifying the values and goals that are most important to you and inspire you. For example, the value of happiness, love, gratitude, kindness, resilience and expressing yourself creatively. You can even define what success means to you personally. Success need not always be defined by material possessions; one of the most important measures of success is the happiness and fulfilment one feels in one's heart. You could consider the ability to stay as pure Awareness, without being pulled and pushed by your thought patterns, as a successful trait too.

Visualize your ideal self: Once you have identified your values and goals, visualize your ideal self, living it out in a positive and fulfilling way. Imagine yourself in different scenarios and situations, and see yourself responding in a way that aligns with your values and goals. Create a visual 'life book'—a picture of how you would like your life to look. Add visuals and details about different aspects of your life, including relationships, career and personal growth. Make it as vivid and as detailed as possible. Whenever possible, open up a page of your life book and vividly create the images in your mind as if you are living the experiences. This will help create the plot of the life story of the character you are playing in the world.

Create a character sketch: Write down a detailed description of your ideal self, including physical characteristics, personality traits and behaviours. Make sure that this description aligns with your values and goals, and that it accurately reflects the person you want to be. Always remember that the character isn't you. The world is a stage and you are the performer. You have to play the role to the best of your capability. In the end, it is just the role you are playing.

Use affirmations: Affirmations are positive statements that can help you to reinforce your positive character sketch. For example, if your character sketch includes the trait of being confident, you can use affirmations such as 'I am confident in my abilities' or 'I trust in my decisions'. Repeat your affirmations regularly and try to incorporate them into your daily routine.

Take action: Once you have created your positive character sketch, take action to bring it to life. Look for opportunities to align your behaviour with your values and goals.

Just as in a lucid dream, the dreamer has a greater degree of self-awareness and cognitive control than in a non-lucid dream, which means they can influence and tweak their dreams, and even change a nightmare into a pleasant dream. Similarly, when we are awakened by the knowledge that we are the Awareness and that the world and the character we are playing are mere appearances in the Awareness, we become capable of creating a better world and a better self in our waking reality.

Let's explore lucid dreaming more. Various techniques can be used to induce lucid dreaming, such as keeping a dream journal, reality checking and mnemonic induction of lucid dreams (MILD). Keeping a dream journal involves writing down your dreams every morning upon waking up. This can help you become more familiar with the patterns and themes of your dreams, which can enhance your ability to recognize when you are dreaming. Reality checking is a technique that involves questioning the reality of your surroundings throughout the day, to train your mind to recognize when it is in a dream state. MILD is a technique that involves setting an intention to become aware that you are dreaming before you fall asleep.

In addition to changing nightmares into positive dreams, lucid dreaming can also be used for other purposes such as problem-solving, self-exploration and personal growth. In the same way that we can actively influence our dreams in a lucid state, when we are awakened by knowledge, we can also create the life we want to live, by taking control of our thoughts, emotions and actions, and actively working towards our goals and aspirations.

Tibetan Buddhism has a rich tradition of dream yoga, which is the practice of using dreams as a tool for spiritual development and awakening through practices such as visualization, recitation of mantras and exploring the nature of reality. Techniques used in Tibetan Buddhism include dream yoga, bardo yoga and lucid dreaming. These techniques help us to develop the ability to remain aware during the dream state. The goal of the practice of yoga of lucid sleep is to use the dream state as a tool for spiritual development and awakening, and to experience a higher state of consciousness, inner light, transcendence and oneness. Dream yoga helps us realize that whatever appears in dreams is mere illusion and therefore can be altered. Illusion simply means it is not appearing in its truest form. The ground of these illusions is Awareness—the light of lights. These illusions borrow our reality and project the world of forms and colours.

While on a solitary retreat at Land of Calm Abiding, I practised the Rainbow Body technique from Tibetan Buddhism. This technique aims to dissolve the physical body into pure light as a sign of advanced spiritual realization and attainment of Buddhahood. When I opened my eyes after the morning meditation, I saw a beautiful rainbow cloud right outside my window in the clear sky. I immediately took a picture of it. This is how the mind creates its own reality. The tendencies or thought patterns that we completely believe in, come to fruition.

If the world that I perceive is the projection of my own mind, then why do we all perceive the same world?

In the dream world, where you create people and objects, all of them experience the same world as you experience, as the dreamer, playing a particular role in the dream. Similarly, in the waking world too, a similar creation is at play. The mind itself projects and experiences the waking world according to the culmination of knowledge it is operating on. The perceiver, the act of perception and the perceived—all rise together at the same time, because they are dependent on each other for their existence; they don't have any inherent reality of their own. That's why they are illusions or dream-like. They only exist because you experience them.

But does our ego not help us survive in this world?

Identifying with the ego makes our life more difficult. The egoic self leads to all kinds of suffering. Old age, disease and death, which are inevitable, scare the egoic self. The inevitable old age, disease and death scare the egoic self. Sooner or later, we realize that the burden we carry of our separate individual selves weigh us down.

Here is a beautiful story of two travellers, named Anil and Om, who were on a long journey by train. Anil was carrying two suitcases on his head, while Om was relaxed, sitting comfortably in his seat, with his luggage stored safely under the seat.

As the train chugged along, Anil's arms began to ache from the weight of his suitcases. He kept shifting the weight from one shoulder to the other, trying to alleviate the pain, but it was of no use. He worked hard to manage the weight of the suitcases, making sure none of them fell. He started to sweat profusely, and his head started to pound. He couldn't help but glance enviously at Om, who was calmly reading a book, with his feet propped up on his seat.

'Why are you carrying your luggage on your head?' asked Om. 'You should put it under your seat, like me. It's much more comfortable.'

Anil replied, 'I always carry my own weight, I don't trust anyone else to do it for me.'

Om smiled and said, 'But the train is carrying your weight too. Just let go of the assumption that you have to carry the weight of all your luggage. The train that is carrying your weight will carry the weight of your luggage too. In truth, it is carrying the weight. You are only assuming that you are carrying the weight anyway. That will not change the fact that the train, in which you are sitting, is carrying the weight of everything placed in it.'

Anil thought about this for a moment and finally, reluctantly, placed his suitcases under the seat. To his surprise, the weight was lifted off his shoulders and he felt a sense of relief wash over him. He took a deep breath and sat back in his seat, feeling the cool breeze on his face. He closed his eyes and let out a sigh of contentment. From that day on, Anil learned to trust in something greater and to surrender his burdens to the universe. He found peace and ease on his journey and was never seen carrying his luggage on his head again.

The story illustrates how, by solidifying our individual self, we insist on carrying our burdens and struggles and then suffer. By trusting in our higher intelligence and dropping the burdens of the egoic self, we can let go of our worries and anxieties and find peace and contentment. Instead of constantly engaging in carrying and managing our problems, we can trust that everything is happening for a reason and that a higher intelligence is taking care of everything.

Even scientifically, the basic physiological processes that are necessary for survival, such as breathing, circulation, digestion and immune function, are regulated by the body's natural systems and occur automatically without conscious effort. The body's systems work together to ensure that oxygen and nutrients are delivered to the cells and that waste products are removed regularly. The immune system works to protect the body from infection and disease. The body's natural healing mechanisms also help repair injury and damage.

It is naive to not recognize the existence of the higher intelligence that pervades the universe.

Mind—the Creator of Our World of Perception

The world we perceive has no inherent reality of its own. The entire universe exists in the mind and the mind exists in the absolute Awareness that we are. In the Awareness, the mind arises which, in turn, gives rise to the world according to the desires. The mind rises as the ego 'I' and the world rises with it, and when the 'I' or mind sets into a deep sleep, the world also ceases to exist. This is an indication that the world we perceive is not an independent reality, but rather a projection of the mind.

So by this logic, nothing in this universe is apart from the Awareness that we are. Everything in this universe is the manifestation of Awareness and we are the Awareness. The Awareness that we are is without beginning and end. We are the constant, in which this transient world appears, persists and disappears in time. All borrow their beingness from that 'I Am' and the 'I Am' shines in everything that exists. Anything conceivable or inconceivable arises in us, the witnessing consciousness.

Does the world really not exist apart from the mind?

The world has no independent existence apart from the Awareness it appears to have. Try to remove the Awareness and see if the world exists.

Here is a good thought experiment: Look at any object that is in front of you. The cause of that object is the Awareness of it. It is made up completely of your Awareness. How? Try to remove your Awareness from the object. Will the object remain? No; if there is no Awareness, we won't be aware of any object, we can't give the object any name and it can't be used for any purpose. One might question this logic with the argument that the object might still exist for someone else and that the object has an inherent existence. But that someone else also exists in your Awareness. Repeat the same experiment with the other person. Everything that exists, exists in you, the Awareness, and is not apart from you. If today, I offer you a billion dollars and ask you to give your Awareness in exchange, you will never take up the offer. If your Awareness is taken away from you, how can you enjoy the world? The money will be worthless to you. The most precious of all things is Awareness because you are the Awareness!

What begins and ends is a mere appearance. The world appears, but has no existence or beingness of its own. The world appears in time and is transitory, and therefore not real.

Take the example of an orange that we see: The image of it is formed in our mind, and that is what we see; we never really see the orange that is outside, but the image of it formed in our visual cortex, a representation of it. The process of visual perception starts with the light which falls on the retina, that is then transformed into electrical signals that travel to the brain. These signals are processed by different regions of the visual cortex, where they are transformed into a representation of the external world that we perceive. This is not a direct copy of the external world but an interpretation of it.

Things cannot exist other than as projections in one's mind. There is no atomically structured external physical reality independent of the mind. The matter that appears so solid can be divided into atoms and subatomic structures, which in itself proves that matter is not as solid as we perceive it. Quantum physics now proves that even the tiniest particle is 99.9999 per cent space.

The Observer Effect is a concept in quantum physics that suggests that the act of observation or measurement can affect the outcome of a physical event. This idea has been used to argue that the mind plays a role in creating our perceived reality. The basic idea is that the mind, through its act of observation, collapses the wave function of a quantum system, determining the outcome of a physical event. In other words, the mind, through its act of observation, plays a role in determining the reality that we perceive.

This idea has been used to argue that our perceptions of the world are not independent of our minds but are instead created by our minds through the act of observation. It suggests that the mind plays a fundamental role in shaping our perceptions and experiences of the world and that the objective reality may not be as independent as we once thought.

Now that we know that the mind is the creator of our world of perception, and we are misidentified with it and our bodies and characters, we can start working on how to stop identifying with these false selves. In the next chapter, I will take you through the possible solutions to this problem we have recognized.

3

Solution: The Road Map to Enlightenment

'Arise, awake, and stop not until the goal is reached.'—Swami Vivekananda

The truth is that we have been eternally free. It is we who do not see the limitlessness of our infinite Self. We have become like a caged bird who has forgotten how to fly. We have gotten used to the cage, though it is utterly restrictive and quite contrary to our real nature of limitlessness. The mind's cage always has an open door of the *Here*, *Now* and *I Am*. A thorough investigation into our fundamental nature as Awareness will set us free.

The inquiry into the 'I' self, that we consider ourselves to be, will lead us to the goal of the true undivided, blissful 'I' Self. The problem at hand is the identification of 'I' with the limiting adjuncts of the body and mind, which seem to be the source of all our problems. Only when 'I' becomes this or that, does 'I' feel limited and have problems. This identification happens because of ignorance about our real nature; once we know who we truly are, all the false identifications will peel off like the dried bark of a tree. This knowledge is a mere pointer. Notice that the goal is ever-attained as the real nature of something does not come and go. It is always present in and through that thing.

Once we have tasted the nectar of our true Self, every time the identification with the body-mind complex will rise, simultaneously witnessing consciousness will rise. Then, we will choose to play the character or remain as witnessing Awareness. Whatever we choose, there will be deep peace and contentment. We will not be looking for satisfaction through the role we are playing in the world, rather the joy and fulfilment that we feel inside will be communicated through the character. If there is a lot of pain arising because of identification, it can be discarded as poison and destroyed at the source of its rise. It does not make any sense to keep identifying with the egoic self, when it is the cause of all our pain.

Let us take the example of a billionaire who has forgotten about his billions and is acting like a beggar. Such a person only needs to be reminded of his wealth for him to be free of the suffering of being a beggar; nothing else is required. He will not go back to being a beggar after the knowledge has dawned. Similarly, once we discover that the solution to all our problems has always been there with us, in us, as us, why will we ever go back to our problems again? As Ramana Maharshi often said, 'Once you have found a cool spot under a tree on a hot, burning summer day, why would you ever leave the shade of the tree for the scorching heat and then come back again and say "Wow! This shade feels good."'

Staying as the witnessing Awareness that transcends all duality, yet permeates through everything that exists, is the ultimate solution to the problem of suffering.

Path of Inquiry (Gyan Yoga)

Before we start our investigation into our real nature, our hearts should be firmly set on the intention of liberating ourselves. We must enter the process of investigation with the purest of intentions and the finest focus.

The process of inquiry is accomplished in two steps: the process of negation and the process of assimilation. This process is mentioned in the *Upanishads* and can be beneficial in cutting through the delusion of *Maya* (the manifested world of names and forms). Let's dive into a few types of investigations and analyses that can help with this process.

1. States of the Mind

We can start with our everyday experience. We go through three states of consciousness every day—waking, dreaming and deep sleep.

In the waking state, we become an individual (waker), experiencing a waking world composed of innumerable forms and names. We, as wakers, use our five senses of sight, smell, sound, taste and touch, as instruments to explore the waking world of names and forms.

Similarly, in the dream state, we take up a dream body and become a dreamer, projecting a dreamworld of experience. We use dream-senses to experience the world of dreams. During the dream state, unless we are lucid dreaming, not for a second do we doubt the reality of the dream world and the dreamer.

During the deep sleep state, the deep sleep world and the deep sleeper are merged in the blankness of deep sleep.

There is a fourth state mentioned in the *Upanishads*, which is the state of an enlightened one. In this state, the individual self and the world of appearances are realized as being the one Awareness. It is not a state of mind, it is the witness of all the mental states with their pairs of knowers and knowns. It is the substratum that enables the mind to project all three worlds. The mind borrows its existence from this pure infinite Awareness, which is our real nature.

Here is a tabulated sketch of this paradigm with the pairs of knowers and knowns in each state:

State of Mind	Knower	Known
Waking	Waker	Waking World
Dreaming	Dreamer	Dream World
Deep Sleep	Deep Sleeper	Darkness/ Blankness
Enlightened (Fourth state)	Awareness	Awareness

The general human population experiences the first three states every day. To get to the truth, and to know our real nature, we need to investigate these three states. This investigation, if followed correctly, will lead us to the truth. This logical investigation leads to psychological benefits; it doesn't resolve our problems but dissolves them altogether.

Owing to ignorance of our real nature, we feel bound by these states and suffer. The inquiry will remove ignorance and help us recognize our infinite nature. Let this investigation take us from the known (suffering/limited self) to the unknown (Bliss/real self).

Is there any waking world apart from you, the waker?

The first aspect of our mind takes the set of the waker and its waking world. The waker is the 'I' self, and the waking world is all the world other than 'me', with people, things, places, books, ideas and knowledge. The whole plethora of real external objects seems to exist of its own accord and 'I', the waker, experiences a material world outside, that seems to exist apart from 'me'.

If we look closely enough at our experience as a waker, we will come to a point where we can appreciate the fact that there is no external world apart from the experiencer. This only requires following our experience. If you remove you, the Awareness, from the equation, can a separate world exist apart from you? If yes, then you won't be aware of it. You might say that other people are still aware of the world, but where are the other people? Are they also not in your Awareness? There is no separate external world apart from you, the waker. Just like you create your dream world, you create your waking world too.

The waker seems to take in or feed on external objects through the outwardly-oriented sense organs. The senses continuously bombard our minds with information about the outer world. Let us closely examine one of these—our sense of sight. Our eyes pick up the visual frequencies of light. When sunlight falls on something, for instance, a green plant, it absorbs all the other colour frequencies, except green, which is reflected back. That's why the plant appears green. This is so intriguing because the plant could have appeared in any other colour but the frequency it did not absorb is the colour in which it appears. After these frequencies are captured by the eyes' lenses, they travel the neural pathway as an electrical signal to the visual cortex, which finally decodes the frequency as a form. Then, we name that form 'the plant'.

We are seeing this form in our minds. So what we are seeing is not what exists outside but an image formed in our own mind. Therefore, it doesn't have any inherent existence apart from the mind that is seeing it. Similarly, all our other senses grasp frequencies and decode them in the mind. The external world only seems to appear; there is no solid external world outside of our mind. Where does this outside demarcation start? If it is all in the mind, where are the inside and the outside?

The sense of touch is very interesting too—it imparts a sense of solidity to the external world. Because something rubs against our touch, we call it solid. But according to quantum physics, matter can exist as a particle or wave, and matter is 99.9999 per cent space; then where is the solidity of the world?

These scientific revelations blur the gap between the waker and the waking world. No separate waker is experiencing a separate, external waking world. The process of understanding this is to first merge the external world into the mental world and then the mental world back into the Awareness that you are.

What happens in a dream state?

The second state, or the dream state, is the biggest grace; it is the clue to solving this riddle. We create and project a dream world of names and forms that we experience as dreamers, with the help of a dream body. All of dreaming is the creation of the mind, using the background of Awareness. Just as the spider spins thread out of itself and again withdraws it back into itself, the mind projects the world out of itself and again resolves it into itself. For instance, imagine you project a desert, with palm trees and a road far, far away, in your dream. There are people around on camels, a lady carrying a pot on her head, and the feeling of thirst and the search for water. The dream thirst can be satisfied by only the dream water. The whole of the world is created in you, by you, and through you. There is no separate world out there but you.

There is not much difference between the dream world and the waking world. If we become aware, we can see how we project this whole world according to the set of tendencies we believe in and want to experience. During lucid dreaming, we can tweak our dreams according to our liking because we are slightly aware and not completely unconscious; similarly, we can tweak our waking world if we have started to awaken to our real conscious nature.

Ignorance is Bliss in the Deep Sleep State

The third state is the state of deep sleep, where there is complete rest, as we are not playing any roles there. We are happily merged into the deepest possible unconsciousness. It is one of the most fulfilling experiences for humans, and we rise rejuvenated, brimming with energy, ready for the next day. Scientists say that if we don't get into a deep sleep, we feel drained and after a few days, we can hardly function. A lack of deep sleep has very harmful effects on our health. There is no separateness here; it is our causal state and very close to the fourth or the enlightened state as there is no duality. However, the seed of ignorance is still present here.

If, by the sword of knowledge, we succeed in cutting through the darkness of ignorance, we enter into what is called the *turiya awastha*, or the fourth state. This state of the mind refers to the enlightened state. 'Turiya' literally means the fourth. Once we enter the fourth state—the state of presence—we see this whole world as the divine play of Awareness, in Awareness, and as Awareness. The world shines forth as the Self. Then there is only infinite bliss; suffering ends and we enter the space of fullness. Everything that appears is auspicious and a dance of bliss!

The investigation into the first three states is the process of negation and the realization of the fourth state is the process of assimilation, where everything is merged back into Awareness and realized as Awareness.

Imagine a person who opens the door of her shop every morning, ready to transact business with the world. She sells and buys, interacts with the customers, and is fully engaged with the external world through the doors of her senses. She is 'the waker', fully aware of her surroundings and herself. As the day comes to an end, this person shuts the shutters of her shop, signalling the end of her interactions with the external world. She goes into another room, where she turns on the TV and watches a show. She is now 'the dreamer', experiencing a different reality through her thoughts and imagination. Finally, when the TV is switched off, this person retires to a third room and tucks herself into bed. She is now in a state of deep rest, where she is not aware of her surroundings or herself. She is 'the deep sleeper', in a state of deep sleep.

This person, whether she is conducting business in her shop, relaxing and watching TV in the other room, or sleeping in the third room, is the same—she is the shopkeeper, the TV watcher and the sleeper. The three rooms and the three roles are just different appearances of the same one person. This one person is the reality.

Our ignorance makes us consider the waking individual as the reality and the world around us as solid and real. We consider the waker as the 'I': 'this is me, this is my life, here are my problems'. But in truth, all the problems and concerns of the waking state disappear when we enter the dream state, and all the good and bad experiences of the dream state disappear when we enter deep sleep.

The one who is experiencing all of these states is the fourth, the pure consciousness, the *Atman*, the observer of all states. This fourth state is always present, underlying the three appearances of waking, dreaming and deep sleep. The fourth state, or pure Awareness, has put on the dress of the waker during the waking state, the dress of the dreamer during the dreaming state, and of the deep sleeper during deep sleep.

The key to realizing ourselves as the one constant that underlies all the three states, of waking, dreaming and deep sleep, is consistent practice and a commitment to self-discovery. It is important to remember that the realization of the true Self is not a destination, but a journey of self-discovery. It is a process of becoming more and more aware of the observer within us, and gradually transcending the states of consciousness, until we realize ourselves as the one constant, pure consciousness.

2. Investigation into the Five Sheaths

The five sheaths, or *koshas*, in Hindu philosophy, refer to the different layers or coverings that surround the true Self or Atman. Another process of investigation is to look into the five sheaths and negate them one by one, to get to the Awareness, the real Self.

The five sheaths covering the real Self are:

1. **The Gross Physical Sheath** (*Annamaya kosha*): This is the outermost layer, made up of the physical body and its organs and systems.
2. **The Energy/Breath Sheath** (*Pranamaya kosha*): This layer is made up of the breath and the life force energy that animates the physical body.
3. **The Thinking Mind Sheath** (*Manomaya kosha*): This layer is made up of the mind, thoughts, emotions, memories and cognitive processes.

4. **The Intellect/Wisdom Sheath** (*Vijnanamaya kosha*): This layer is made up of the intellect and the ability to discriminate, reason and make judgements. This is where all understanding arises.

5. **The Bliss Sheath** (*Anandamaya kosha*): This is the innermost layer, closest to the true Self, or Atman, which is pure consciousness and eternal bliss.

The goal of spiritual practices is to transcend these five sheaths, and realize the true Self, or Atman, which is beyond the five sheaths. This realization allows us to see that these five sheaths are not who we truly are, but rather, they are just temporary coverings that obscure our true nature.

The first sheath is made up of food and that's why it is called Annamaya (literally, the layer made of food). We are not the physical body. The body never claims our possession, but we claim the possession of the physical body. How can the possessor of the body be the body? The consciousness is always on our side or internal to the body. How can something external to us be us?

Earlier in this book, we did an interesting experiment, wherein you raise your hand and say 'Hi' to the hand, and then imagine the hand saying 'Hi' back to you. This simple experiment demonstrates that the conscious Self is internal to the body. We can apply this process to all the other sheaths. Are you aware of the breath or is the breath aware of you? Are you aware of your thought or is the thought aware of you? Are you aware of the understanding or is the understanding aware of you? Are you aware of the rejuvenation experienced during deep sleep or is the darkness of deep sleep aware of the joy?

However, it is important to note that even though we transcend these five sheaths, we are still eminent in these five sheaths, as they will lose their existence in our absence. These five sheaths are the instruments that allow us to experience the world; without them, we would not be able to interact with the world. They are necessary for our existence in this world, but they should not be mistaken for our true selves.

3. The Analysis of the Seer and the Seen

This investigation is taken from *Drig Drishya Vivek*, an introductory text of the *Vedanta*.

We have to start this process of investigation with three discerning factors: The seer cannot be the seen, as the subject can never be the object. The seer is one, the seen are many. The seer remains relatively unchanged, the seen changes.

The forms of the world are seen by the eyes. The forms are nothing but colours and shapes. The forms are the seen, the eyes are the seer. The eyes are not the forms they see. The eyes (as the organ of sight) are one and the forms are many—like books, trees, tables, etc. The eyes remain relatively unchanged; the seen keeps changing.

In the next step of this investigation, the eyes become the seen and the mind is the seer. The mind is one, and the conditions of the eyes become many; for example, my eyes are open, my eyes are closed. The mind remains relatively unchanged, the eyes change, like maybe the eyes need glasses, or maybe they have perfect vision.

In the final step, the mind becomes the seen and the witnessing consciousness becomes the seer. The witnessing consciousness remains one, the mind with its thought patterns is many. It is said that we have close to 10,000 thoughts in a day. The witnessing consciousness remains unchanged, whereas the thoughts are continuously changing.

We, as witnessing consciousness, can never become an object of perception or inference. We are the non-dual, unattached, self-luminous existence-consciousness-bliss.

The seer is not the seen, but is the seen different from the seer?

To establish non-duality, it is crucial to understand this. As a seer, as the witnessing consciousness, we are apart from the seen, the observed. But the observed, which lacks inherent existence of its own, is not apart from the seen. Two things, for instance, can be seen separately if they have an independent, separate existence. A book in front of you is separate from a glass in front of you. They can be shown separately and one's existence is not dependent on the other. But can anything be experienced apart from Awareness? Awareness is primordial and the basis of any experience. Without Awareness, there can be no experience.

Let's take the example of a clay pot: The first step is to observe a pot. The second step is to recognize the material cause of the pot being clay. The third step is to investigate the pot—the inside and the outside of it are clay. The upper and lower part of the pot is also clay. Then what exactly is the pot? The name, the form and the function (the immaterial aspects) are called the pot.

Apart from the clay, the pot has no inherent existence of its own. If I take away the clay, will you be left with a pot? Can you call it something? Can it be used for a purpose like storing water? The answer is No. The pot cannot exist without the clay. The fourth step is to realize that nothing new has been produced. The pot is nothing but clay, so the pot is not different from the clay, so nothing new has been created.

Now let's apply this example to ourselves and the world of our perception: The first step is to look around and see the world. The second step is to recognize the material cause as Awareness. The third step is to investigate the world. If you remove the Awareness from the world, will there be an observed world of appearance? If I say you can give me your Awareness and you can have the world, will you make that trade? No, because without your Awareness, how can you experience the world? The world cannot exist apart from Awareness. It has a borrowed reality. In the fourth step, nothing new has been created. The world of forms we experience is nothing but Awareness.

This process of investigation can be applied to the mental world of thoughts as well and merge the mind back into Awareness, where it borrows its existence from. See the world, the mind as Awareness—the Self that you are!

4. The Emptiness of Emptiness Technique

The Emptiness of Emptiness technique pertains to the *Prasangika* view within the *Madhyamaka*, which is one of the four schools of Buddhist philosophy. According to this view, the existence of an object, such as a table, is merely a label that is assigned by the mind, and it is not an inherent aspect of the object itself. In other words, the table has no inherent existence of its own, and any sense of solidity or substantiality that we attribute to it is illusory. This technique involves contemplating the emptiness of emptiness itself, or the ultimate lack of inherent existence in all phenomena. By recognizing and experiencing this emptiness, we can let go of our attachments and delusions, and achieve a deeper state of understanding.

Let's follow this example closely; there are four parts: When we walk into a room, we see a table and our brain creates an image of it. We, then, call it a table. However, the table is not just the legs, the base or any other individual part. Even all of these parts together are not the table.

So, where is the table then? The table exists in the room, in the form of the legs, the base, and the other parts. This is why we believe there is a table in the room. However, the name, form and function of the table are not real because they don't have their own inherent existence.

The example actually refers to a concept in Buddhist philosophy known as 'emptiness'. According to this philosophy, everything we perceive is not a fixed, permanent entity in and of itself, but rather a collection of parts or aggregates that come together temporarily to form what we perceive as an object or phenomenon.

In the case of the table, we perceive it as a single, solid object, but in reality, it is made up of individual parts like the legs, the base and the tabletop. None of these parts, on their own, can be considered the table. Even all of the parts together do not constitute the table in its entirety.

The reason we believe there is a table in the room is that the parts are arranged in such a way as to create the appearance of a table. We give it a name and a function, but these are not inherent qualities of the object itself. They are concepts that we apply to the object based on our perceptions and experiences.

In Buddhist philosophy, this idea of emptiness applies not just to physical objects, but to all phenomena, including thoughts, emotions and even the self. The concept of emptiness is meant to challenge our usual way of thinking and encourage us to see the world and ourselves in a more nuanced and interconnected way.

Now let's apply this example to see how 'I', the knower, the false egoic self exists: Our body is not the 'I', nor is our mind. The association of body and mind is the base to be labelled 'I'. When we say 'my body and my mind', or refer to the group of aggregates as 'mine', we can see that the 'I' is the possessor and they are the possessions.

The possessor can't be the possessed. Therefore, it is clear that the body and mind or their aggregates are not the 'I'. Neither are these separately the 'I' nor when grouped, are they the 'I'. We can find no 'I' in this body and mind. However, that doesn't mean that there is no 'I'. The 'I' that exists is nothing other than that which is merely imputed by the mind in dependence upon the aggregates.

The ego-made self is a mental construct, with no real 'I' there. The 'I' is empty of existing on its own. When somebody talks ill about us, we normally think that they are hurting this 'I'. We then get angry and want to harm them. If someone praises us, we think that they are praising this real 'I'. We feel good about it and become attached to the person.

We work so hard all our lives to defend or aggrandize this egoic self. However, the object that appears to us, and which we thoroughly believe in, does not exist. The 'I' existing by itself is a complete hallucination—it's empty. Thinking of the emptiness of the 'I' brings the understanding of its dependent arising.

How can we apply the emptiness technique in our daily lives?

After the knowledge of the 'I' being empty arises, when somebody criticizes or tries to harm us, it is akin to somebody criticizing or harming us in a dream. There is no subject—to be harmed—and there is no object—somebody trying to cause harm. Even though these situations might appear to exist, as they are fundamentally empty, there is no point in getting angry.

By realizing the nature of the egoic self, we eliminate the ignorance of its true existence. We then eliminate all the delusion that arises from it, viz., Desire, Anger, Pride, Attachment, Jealousy. The clinging to the egoic self loosens and the death-grasp we have on our body-mind pries open. As we have discovered the cause of suffering and eradicated the egoic self, all true suffering ceases. Since there's no cause of suffering left within our consciousness, no ignorance or even a seed of it—it's impossible for suffering to arise again.

All the above described investigations and analyses pertaining to the path of inquiry are to be listened to or read, and contemplated again and again until the full realization dawns. Until and unless all the doubts cease, the inquiry should continue. There will come a time when the unquestioned conviction will rise from the depths of our being, which shall lead to the cessation of all our sufferings.

Path of Psychic Control (Raja Yoga)

Once you have developed insight by way of inquiry, it is time to absorb your mind in the Self and calmly abide by *it*. And that's when meditation becomes very useful. Until the Self is realized and even after the Self is realized, if we want to experience bliss, the training of the mind is essential. The mind needs to be purified by all means necessary. No matter what thoughts arise in your mind, keep rejecting them and keep coming back to Awareness, utilizing the 'I Am-ness', the present moment, breath or mindfulness.

All these techniques serve only one purpose and that is to purify the mind. A purified mind is not separate from Awareness, as a purified mind's nature is to dwell in and as the all-encompassing Awareness. If we examine our mind closely, we see how it creates a thought and in no time, a chain of thoughts is created. Say, you are sitting at a table and reading a book but suddenly, a thought crosses your mind that you need to buy groceries, and then you think of the grocery store and the last time you met someone at the grocery store. You start thinking about the person, then the vacation they went on, then about the beauty of the place. You get the drift—this is how chains of thoughts are formed in your mind one after the other.

The point is to unclutch from these thought patterns using any of the techniques. Bringing back the focus to the present. Many personal problems, including managing anger, lust, jealousy and so on, can be solved by this process.

Managing negative emotions is just the offshoot; the main purpose is the joy of being. In many ancient scriptures, it is written that the highest joy one can experience is the joy of being and if you haven't experienced it, all other joys sooner or later become limitations. For example, today you want a beautiful car. But once you have purchased the car, you start thinking about the loan payments, and then the maintenance and insurance. Then, you start worrying that if it gets into an accident you will have to get it fixed, and if it damages some other car, you will have to talk on the phone with the insurance guys for hours. It is a lot of work and can take away peace of mind.

The bliss of being is always available to us, and the more we reside in that state of being, the more it grows and brings joy to our lives. As we continue to practise techniques such as meditation, mindfulness and self-reflection, we begin to develop a deeper understanding of our true nature as pure Awareness. This understanding can lead to a shift in perspective, where we see ourselves as a whole, already complete, rather than as separate and isolated individuals. As we continue to reside in this state of being, we may find that we can experience joy and contentment in even the most mundane activities. For example, while walking or doing other routine activities, we may find ourselves filled with an intense sense of happiness and contentment that is difficult to contain. This is because, in this state of being, we are no longer focused on external sources of happiness but rather, we are finding joy in the present moment and the simple things of life. We are not seeking happiness in external things, but in our true nature as the Awareness, and that is where true and lasting happiness can be found.

It doesn't take any effort to give up something. Nothing has to be done; 'this is not me and it is not mine'—this clarity can help us drop the deepest of our desires. Even though this giving up of desires is one of the easiest tasks, we can't seem to do it, because we have attached ourselves to them. Our desires and our achievements have started defining who we are. On the other hand, to acquire something, we have to work very hard, and put in a lot of effort. Our conditioning pushes us towards certain desires; we work very hard to get them, to finally realize that they have left us emptier than before. And the fear of losing something that we have already acquired is another reason for our restlessness. Our possessions are like heavy rocks, tied to us, weighing us down. We willingly bind ourselves and then wonder what happened to our freedom. If you are attached or holding on to something, the thing you are holding on to is attached to you too. You can't complain; just let go.

Here is a story of a curious monkey who loved to explore his surroundings. One day, while wandering through the jungle, he came across a jar filled with ripe, juicy bananas. Without hesitation, he reached into the jar to grab a banana. But as he pulled it out, his hand got stuck in the jar because he was holding the banana.

The jar belonged to a farmer who grew bananas as his main crop. The farmer saw the monkey trying to take his bananas and started thrashing him. But the monkey was unwilling to let go of the banana. He held on tight, despite the thrashing and the pain. If only the monkey had let go of the banana, he could have easily escaped the farmer's wrath. But his desire to eat the banana kept him stuck to the jar.

We might laugh at the monkey, but we are doing the same thing. Because of our attachments, we are taking the 'thrashing' of our mind in the form of compulsive desires. If only we learn to let go of these compulsive thoughts, we can find peace and freedom in the ever-present Awareness.

We have to patiently keep training the mind until it drops all its attachments and settles down in pure Awareness. The purification process might take time but we have to keep at it, without giving up. The only thing that is required is a strong will to overcome the pain. The poet Tulsidas had said, 'Repeated up and down motion of a soft rope can make a mark even on a huge stone. Similarly, by repeated practice, even a man of ignorance can become a man of knowledge, a fully enlightened one.'

There is a very inspiring story in the *Vedas* of a sparrow who laid her eggs at the shore of a vast ocean. But fate was not kind to the little bird, as a big wave came and swept her eggs out into the sea. The sparrow was devastated and asked the ocean to return her eggs, but the ocean paid no heed to her plea. Determined to get her eggs back, the sparrow began to pick out the water in her small beak, one drop at a time, to dry up the entire ocean. Narad Muni was passing by and saw the little bird struggling for hours, taking out a drop of water in her beak and throwing it away. Narad told her that it was an impossible feat and that her beak was too small to throw away all the ocean water. But the sparrow paid no attention and asked Narad Muni to leave. She said that at least the water she had thrown away has reduced some of the ocean, and that she would continue doing so, whatever time and effort it would take. Narad Muni informed Garuḍa (the gigantic bird carrier of Lord Viṣṇu) about the sparrow's determination. Moved by the sparrow's plight, Garuḍa flew to the ocean's shore to see the determined bird for himself. Garuḍa was impressed by the sparrow's determination and promised to help her. He confronted the ocean and threatened to dry it up himself if it did not return the sparrow's eggs. The ocean, fearing Garuḍa's power, returned the eggs to the sparrow. So, if your determination is strong and you have an iron-strong will to not give up until the goal is reached, the higher power's grace also falls on you and starts helping you.

Spiritual practice is the repeated assertion of willpower. A simple and honest longing for the truth is enough to take us to the shore. It is the true intention that matters; the path gets created on its own. The courage to continue, to repeat, to endure and persevere, even in the face of boredom and despair, is non-negotiable. A sincere commitment arises towards the practice when there is a genuine search for freeing oneself of bondage. When one has had enough suffering, then these become the practices using which you can set yourself free of all the struggles and suffering. Thus, often, spiritual practitioners are called 'Dheera'—the patient and courageous ones.

Try to follow one of the techniques of psychic control, described below, till its fruition. Multiple techniques can also be followed, depending on the temperament of the mind and the situation. The main purpose of these techniques is to enter a thought-free state.

1. Tuning the Mind to the Presence of Beingness

The mind should be immersed in the sense of 'I Am' that exists prior to the thoughts. The meditation on the Source of 'I am' should be done incessantly. The mind should be brought back and held by effort on the sense of existence and consciousness.

Ask yourself, do you exist? The answer will arise—yes. Then dive deep and see from where this sense of existence rises in the body. Tracing the Source will take you to the heart, which is beyond the realm of body and mind. And the real Self will draw you and you will soon be absorbed in the Self. You can repeat this time and again and experience the luminosity of the Self.

Develop a sense of curiosity about what your next thought is going to be. And then, with full attention, keep watching your mind for the next thought it is going to produce. Be like a cat, who is completely alert and curious to see when the mouse will come out of its hole. When you experiment like this, you will experience 'beingness' or presence. That is 'I Amness', when you are consciously cut from the stream of your thinking.

When the mind is stabilized in the 'I Am', we enter an indescribable, transcendental state. A constant effort should be made to stay with the sense of 'I Am'. Inquire from where this emerges and notice it attentively with a quiet and concentrated mind. The sense of 'I Am' is ever available and constantly with us, only we have attached several other conjunctions to it, like the body, thoughts, ideas, feelings, material possessions and so on. Identification with these conjunctions is the cause of our suffering.

Just like beauty, love, joy or anything subtle and fundamental, the sense of 'I Amness' cannot be described. But it can be experienced and felt. Even the *Bible* mentions 'I Am is that I Am and "I am" is the way'. Feel this sense of

'I Am' as a pure white light expanding from your heart to the whole of your body, filling your body completely. As you stay with this sense of beingness, the outer limits of your body will start to vanish and the beingness will expand and pervade the whole space. Everything will happen in this state of being. Everything and everyone will become part of it. All that is required to happen will happen from this state of absolute stillness and peace. All anxieties will leave you as you won't feel any sense of separateness.

2.   Tuning the Mind to the Breath

The breath is the bridge between the physical body and the subtle body—it is neither physical nor subtle. Since the breath has both aspects in it, it can work to control the mind as well as energize the body.

In Buddhism, the practice of mindfulness of breath, also known as '*anapana-sati*' is one of the fundamental techniques to train the mind. The Buddha taught this technique as a means to develop concentration, which is one of the essential factors in the path to enlightenment. The practice of mindfulness of breath is considered to be one of the most effective ways to bring the mind under control and cultivate a sense of inner peace. There is a whole section of Pranayama in yoga too, dedicated to controlling the breath, thus controlling the mind and body.

By focusing the mind on the breath, one can learn to observe the fluctuations of the mind and develop a sense of inner calm and equanimity. We can practise this technique at any time and in any situation—whether at work, during meals, during leisure activities, or even during moments of stress or conflict. By focusing the mind on the breath and disconnecting from thought patterns, we can immediately find peace and tranquillity.

In addition to its spiritual benefits, mindfulness of breath also has several physical and mental health benefits. Modifying our breathing patterns can help us to regulate emotions and reduce feelings of anger and passion. Slow and deep breathing can activate the parasympathetic nervous system, which is responsible for the 'rest and digest' response in our body. This can lead to a decrease in heart rate and blood pressure, as well as an increase in feelings of relaxation and calm.

Holding the breath in for a few seconds and then gently letting it go can further enhance these effects. This technique, known as 'breathing retention' or 'kumbhaka' in yoga, can increase lung capacity, improve oxygenation and circulation, and strengthen the diaphragm and other respiratory muscles.

Research has shown that mindfulness of breath can have a positive impact on a variety of health conditions, including anxiety, depression, chronic pain and high blood pressure. It can also improve sleep quality, boost the immune system, and help to manage stress and negative emotions. We should be mindful of the breath, but not force it. It should be a natural process. If it becomes forced, it can cause more problems than benefits.

3. Tuning the Mind to the Here and Now

Bringing the mind to the here and now is yet another technique to train the mind to come out of its incessant chattering. This technique helps in dropping the psychological time of the past and future, and tuning our mind to the present moment. Though we are always in the here and now, often our minds are preoccupied with thoughts of the past and future, which can lead to feelings of anxiety and stress. The present moment is called the present or a gift for a reason: in the here and now is the space and the time where we can feel the presence fully. We are always in the here and now anyway, so why not accept and embrace it fully? Whatever is rising in the here and now, the situation, the people, be in no conflict with them. Their existence is synonymous with the here and now, so why fight them? Trying to resist them won't make them disappear, so accepting them is wisdom. Trying to resist or fight against the present moment only causes mental conflict and suffering, whereas accepting it fully is a sign of maturity. By accepting and embracing the present moment and whatever is arising within it, we can find inner peace and learn to live in harmony with the present moment.

Let's have a closer look at what we call the 'present time'. We can divide time into three parts: the time that is gone in the past, the time that is yet to come in the future, and somewhere in between lies the time in the present. The present is elusive. What we call the present becomes the past by the time we point at it. There is hardly anything remaining that we can truly call present. We find that between the past and the future, there is an extremely thin line, something that cannot withstand analysis and remain as the present. Time, in essence, is indivisible if we try to maintain a single point but if we do divide time, then there is hardly any present remaining. Past is past in relation to the now, future is future in relation to the now. Your own presence is the portal to the now, the present.

Conventional time has a purpose in this world of perception, but it has no role to play in the realization of the Self. The concept of time is a human construct, and time doesn't necessarily exist in the same way when it comes to understanding and experiencing the true nature of Self.

The present moment is the key to understanding and transcending the illusory nature of time and our limited existence. By focusing on the present moment, we can break free from the mental constructs of the past and future and find inner stillness and peace.

Applying Mindfulness in All Actions

Your attention should be completely directed to the activity you are involved in. So, for instance, when you're cutting vegetables, focus on picking the knife, the feeling of it slicing through the peel, the flesh of the vegetable, the smell of the vegetable you are cutting, the sound of cutting a vegetable and the sensation of the hand holding the knife. Be completely present with all the senses.

Applying mindfulness in all actions is a powerful way to be aware and live in the present moment. When you are fully engaged in an activity and give it your complete attention, you can experience it more deeply and authentically. By directing your attention to the specific details of the action, you become fully present and mindful of the experience. By being fully present in this way, psychological thought patterns related to the past or future are less likely to arise, and you can experience a sense of inner peace and stillness. This approach can be applied to any activity, whether it's washing dishes, taking a walk or even something as simple as brushing your teeth.

It takes practice and patience to develop the ability to be fully mindful of all actions, but with consistent effort, it can become a natural part of one's life. Being mindful is like walking a razor's edge; our mind will wander. This is not a problem, it's just the nature of the mind. When you notice that your mind has wandered away, gently bring it back to the present moment and the action at hand.

Path of Surrender and Love (Bhakti Yoga)

When we understand ourselves as pure Awareness, it can lead to a sense of surrender to the higher Self. As we realize that the world and all its experiences are simply appearances within Awareness, we can let go of our attachment to the individual self and its desires. This process of surrendering the ego can be seen as an act of wisdom, as it allows us to align with our true nature of the Self. The path of surrender, or Bhakti Yoga, involves devotion and surrender to our higher Self. Everything is understood to be the doing of the higher Self. Only He, the Divine, exists—our sole responsibility is to remember this. Make this life story about just him and you. Every incident should be seen in the light of him trying to communicate with you. All your actions should be an act performed to show your love towards him as if you are trying to please him with your actions and goodness. Whenever a sense of a separate 'I' and 'mine' arises, keep offering the egoic self and its actions to the higher Self and keep accepting all results as his *prasad* or grace.

The path of Bhakti Yoga cultivates a sense of love and devotion towards the divine, which can lead to a deeper understanding of one's true nature as pure Awareness and the dissolution of the ego. The path of knowledge and the path of surrender can be synonyms in the sense that in order to surrender the ego, one needs to have a deep understanding of one's true nature as Awareness and the impermanence of the individual self. And for a realization of oneself as the Awareness, one has to have a deep sense of longing for freedom from suffering and to realize the divine truth.

1. Recognizing the Presence of Divine/Higher Consciousness

The egoic self has to give way to the higher Self when it realizes its own limitations. It is because of the higher Self, the great compassion, that space, the sun, the five elements, and the dream and deep sleep exist in this creation, so that we can contemplate them and experience reality.

Imagine that the entire creation is a gift from the divine to you, an expression of divine love. Envision a state of divine love, where every aspect of the world has been carefully crafted by God to convey infinite love and care for you. The sun rises in the sky, filling the world with its warmth and light, while the moon and stars twinkle and shine in the night sky, delighting your heart. From the blooming of flowers to the changing of seasons, from the colours of a beautiful sunset to the hues of a butterfly—all of this has been created by God to bring a smile to your face.

God takes many forms to fill your heart with joy, love, wonder and awe. He is the whole universe, watching over every moment of your life. He became the womb that nourished and carried you, the first hand that held you when you were born, the breasts that fed you, and the arms that cuddled you and provided you with warmth. Through everything, God's love shines through, offering you comfort, support and a sense of wonder and mystery that can fill your life with meaning and purpose.

Open your eyes and see that this is the truth; the world is no other way. Recognizing this will only fill your heart with gratitude. Everything that happens in your life, any situation, any person that comes into your life, is a message from God. You might tell me that not all situations or people are pleasant, but your attitude determines what you make of the situation and people. If you take them as messengers of God, you will be able to convert anything into a blessing. You will see a tough situation as a challenge offered by God to train your mind to become finer and purer.

This whole life will be like a *homa* (a fire ritual) you are performing at every moment, with everything offered in the fire of love. Love purifies you and loving the higher self (God) works as an emotional catharsis. This homa involves offering all aspects of oneself, including thoughts, actions and emotions, to the divine in a spirit of love and devotion. This can help purify the mind and emotions and bring one closer to the higher Self. Additionally, the act of offering is a form of emotional cleansing, as it allows us to release and transform negative emotions and patterns that may have been stored from past experiences, either from one's own life or inherited from ancestors.

The gift of loving God is a pure mind that is mostly filled with joy, love and gratitude. Love is often the foundation of spiritual practice, as it allows one to connect with the divine and with others in a deeper and more meaningful way. Gratitude, on the other hand, is often seen as the natural response to the blessings and abundance that life offers. When one is able to cultivate a sense of love and gratitude, it brings a sense of peace and contentment, and fosters a deeper sense of connection with oneself, others and the world around us.

It is generally more difficult for a mind that is pure and filled with love and gratitude to be bogged down by negative emotions. A sense of love and gratitude can act as a shield against negative emotions such as anger, fear and resentment. This is because when the mind is focused on positive emotions, it is less likely to become fixated on negative thoughts and feelings. When one is able to let go of negative emotions through practices like emotional catharsis, it becomes easier to maintain a state of inner peace and balance.

A pure mind can be seen as a state of mindfulness and non-attachment where one is able to observe thoughts and emotions without getting caught up in them. It can also be described as a state of equanimity, where one is able to remain calm and stable in the face of life's challenges.

A pure mind doesn't mean that one will be immune to negative emotions; it's just that the negative emotions will not last and not affect one's overall well-being as much. Negative emotions may still arise in a pure mind, but the key difference is that they do not linger or take hold the way they would in a mind that is not focused on love and gratitude. When negative emotions do arise in a pure mind, they are more likely to be acknowledged, felt, and then released, instead of being suppressed or dwelled upon.

A pure mind is also more resilient and adaptable, so it can process negative emotions in a healthy way, allowing the individual to learn from them and grow. In this way, a pure mind can be seen as a state of mental and emotional balance, where one is able to navigate the ups and downs of life with greater ease and equanimity.

Once oneness is established with the divine, the whole of creation becomes one with you as you can't find yourself apart from the divine. This oneness leads to a profound sense of interconnectedness and unity with the whole of creation. You no longer feel like an isolated island separate from everything around you. This can be incredibly beautiful and magnificent, as it can bring a sense of peace, fulfilment and purpose. Then one's actions are guided by the understanding that everything is interconnected and non-separate from the Awareness in which they are rising. This understanding brings a sense of compassion and empathy for others, as one recognizes that we are all connected and that the suffering of others is also our own suffering.

The mirror neuron system in the brain is thought to play a role in this process, as it allows us to understand and empathize with the emotions and experiences of others. This system enables us to 'mirror' the emotions and actions of others, which allows us to understand and respond to their experiences in a more empathetic and compassionate way.

The higher intelligence has put this system in place to help us understand the interconnectedness of all things and to foster compassion and empathy for others, as it allows us to see the world through others' eyes and to understand the impact of our actions on others.

In this age, the emphasis on individuality and the need to establish oneself as separate and better than others can be toxic and unhealthy. It can lead to a sense of competition and a compulsion to prove oneself different and special, which can produce stress and anxiety. This can also create a sense of disconnection and isolation from others. The focus on competition and individual achievement is often at odds with our organic brotherhood and unity. It is important to remember that we are all interrelated, and what affects one affects all. We are all part of the same larger whole, and our individual actions have an impact on the collective.

The ancient *rishis*, who were considered to be spiritual leaders, gave credit to God for the greatest teachings, a reminder that the teachings and knowledge were not their own but a gift from the divine. The emphasis was on humility and interconnectedness. In today's world, the emphasis is on copyrights and patents, a different world view where the focus is on individual achievement and proprietary knowledge.

The natural world is an awe-inspiring masterpiece painted by the creator of the universe, revealing a reflection of the divine. The beauty and complexity of nature are meant to be appreciated by those who have the eye to see them. One of the most striking examples of the divine signature in the natural world is the Fibonacci series, a mathematical pattern found throughout nature. This perfect ratio is achieved by adding the two previous numbers in the series to obtain the next number, starting with 0 and 1. The resulting sequence is 0, 1, 1, 2, 3, 5, 8, 13, 21 and so on. This ratio is present in the spiral patterns of shells, the branching of trees and the arrangement of leaves on a stem, representing a divine proportion that reflects the beauty and harmony of the universe.

Another example of the divine signature in nature is the Mandelbrot set, a fractal pattern that appears in many forms such as coastlines, mountain ranges and the branching patterns of trees. This pattern is generated by iterating a simple formula with complex numbers, resulting in an intricate design that appears infinitely complex, yet is created by a simple set of rules.

The natural world also reflects the divine in the diversity and interdependence of life in ecosystems, where every organism plays a unique role in maintaining balance and harmony. Additionally, the harmony and balance of the solar system, where planets and celestial bodies move in perfect orbits, and the gravitational pull of each body maintains the balance of the entire system, is another reflection of the divine order.

The beauty of nature in all its forms, from the grandeur of mountain ranges to the delicate beauty of flowers, offers examples of divine creativity and beauty. Furthermore, the human body and its complex systems, from the intricacies of the brain to the workings of the heart, all reveal divine intelligence and wisdom.

Lastly, the phenomenon of bioluminescence, which is the ability of certain living organisms to produce light, is another example of the signature of the divine in the natural world. This phenomenon is found in many marine creatures, such as jellyfish and plankton, and is believed to play a role in communication, camouflage and attracting prey. The hexagonal shapes found in many natural forms, such as honeycombs, snowflakes and the basalt columns that form in volcanic rock, are believed to reflect the efficiency and economy of nature, allowing for the maximum use of space and resources.

All these examples showcase the presence of a higher power who has created and who maintains the harmony, balance and beauty of the universe. This understanding brings a sense of awe and wonder at the beauty and complexity of the universe and reminds us that everything is interconnected and that we are all part of the same larger whole.

2. Personal Connection with the Divine

The path of love is often seen as the most direct and beautiful way to connect with the divine, as it is based on the cultivation of positive emotions such as love, gratitude and devotion. The path itself is often seen as being as beautiful and fulfilling as the goal, as the process of cultivating love and connection with the divine can bring a sense of joy and inner peace in itself. As we continue to deepen our connection with the divine and with the world around us, the path of love makes life's journey beautiful.

In the path of Bhakti or devotion, establishing a personal relationship with the divine is considered to be important because it helps the devotee to connect with God on a deeper level and to experience greater intimacy and closeness. There are several types of relationships that can be established with the divine, including:

Mother: This relationship is characterized by a sense of nurturing and protection. The devotee sees God as a loving mother who cares for and protects them. This relationship is often associated with feelings of safety and security.

Father: This relationship is characterized by a sense of authority and guidance. The devotee sees God as a wise and loving father who guides and advises them. This relationship is often associated with feelings of respect and obedience.

Friend: This relationship is characterized by a sense of companionship and mutual understanding. The devotee sees God as a close friend with whom they can share their thoughts and feelings. This relationship is often associated with feelings of trust and intimacy.

Servant: This relationship is characterized by a sense of humility and submission. The devotee sees themselves as a servant of God, who exists to serve and worship God. This relationship is often associated with feelings of humility and devotion.

Child: Seeing the divine as one's own child is a unique relationship that can be established in the path of bhakti or devotion. It is characterized by feelings of love, protection and nurturing. In this relationship, the devotee sees God as their own child and feels a sense of responsibility for the well-being and care of God. This relationship can be expressed through acts of service, such as cooking and cleaning for the temple or God, or through acts of devotion such as singing lullabies to God or carrying God in a procession as a parent carries a child. This type of relationship can be important because it allows the devotee to experience God in a new and personal way, and it can also deepen the devotion and connection with God. It can also help the devotee to cultivate qualities such as compassion, selflessness and humility, as they are constantly working for the betterment of the divine child. Additionally, this relationship can also be seen as a representation of the idea that God is not separate from the devotee, but is rather an extension of the devotee's own self. It can also reflect the idea that God is infinite and present in all creation, including one's own child.

Beloved: The 'Beloved' relationship with the divine is characterized by a deep and intense love and devotion, and is often associated with feelings of longing and yearning to be close to God. This relationship is considered to be one of the most intimate and personal of all the relationships that can be established with the divine in the path of devotion. This relationship encompasses elements of all the other relationships, in the sense that it contains elements of filial love as in the 'mother' and 'father' relationships, companionship as in the 'friend' relationship, humility as in the 'servant' relationship, and the sense of nurturing and protection as in the 'child' relationship. In the 'beloved' relationship, the devotee sees God as their ultimate love and desire, to the point that their love for God is so all-consuming that it can be compared to the love of a lover. It can be expressed through acts of devotion, such as reciting love poetry, singing devotional songs and meditating on God's divine qualities. The beloved relationship can be seen as the ultimate goal of Bhakti Yoga, as it represents the highest level of intimacy and connection with the divine. It is considered to be the most complete and fulfilling of all the relationships, as it encompasses all the other relationships and leads to the ultimate realization of the oneness of the devotee and God.

Each of these relationships is important in the path of bhakti, as they offer different perspectives on the nature of God and the devotee's relationship with God. Ultimately, the most important aspect of any relationship with the divine is the level of devotion and connection that is established between the devotee and God.

On this path, we feel a constant sense of protection and guidance, as we never feel alone in our journey, knowing that God is always with us. We cultivate a sense of humility, service and surrender, as we recognize the infinite nature of God and our own smallness in comparison. A personal relationship with the divine is considered to be a means to ultimate union with the Higher Self, which is considered the ultimate goal of the path of love and surrender. Overall, establishing a personal relationship with the divine helps us in living a more fulfilling and meaningful life, filled with joy and ecstasy.

3. Praying and Communicating with the Divine

The divine is not separate from us; it is the higher Self or inner guide. So when we talk to the divine, we are in fact communicating with our own higher Self and gaining clarity and guidance from it. We can share everything with the higher Self as if we are talking to a friend or someone very close to us. This helps to create a sense of intimacy and connection with the divine and makes it easier to open up and share our thoughts, feelings and struggles. When we talk to the divine as if it were a friend, we can express ourselves more freely and honestly, and we may find that we are better able to receive guidance and support from the divine. Remember that the divine is always listening, even when we think it isn't. And it's good to look for signs of how the divine communicates with us. It could be through a sudden realization, a synchronistic event, a dream, a message from a friend or any other way that the divine chooses to communicate. It's important to be open and receptive to these signs and to trust that the divine is working in our lives in ways that may not always be immediately obvious. Quantum Physics reveals that the universe is a holistic and interconnected system where the observer and the observed are not separate entities. This has led to the idea that the universe is a self-organizing system and that there is an underlying intelligence that governs the behaviour of matter and energy. So, not believing in an intelligent universe can be old school and unwise.

Ultimately, the key to effective communication with the divine is to approach it with an open and sincere heart and to trust that the divine is always listening and working in our lives for our highest good. Prayers are the most effective and powerful way of communicating with the Divine. Like letters written to a friend, prayers can be personal, intimate and heartfelt expressions of one's deepest thoughts, feelings and desires. They can be used to express gratitude, ask for help, guidance, forgiveness or blessings, or simply connect with the divine. Prayers can be recited alone or in a group, and can be spoken or sung. They can be formal or informal and can be recited from memory or read from a book. They can be in the form of words, songs, mantras or even acts of devotion, like prostrations or offerings. They can be personalized according to the individual's preference, culture and tradition, and can be adapted to suit one's own spiritual needs. Prayers can be recited at any time and in any place and can be a powerful tool for gaining inner peace, clarity of mind and spiritual growth. Prayers are considered to be a way of opening oneself up to the divine and allowing the divine to enter one's life. They can help to bring a sense of connection with the divine. When one prays with an open and sincere heart, the divine always listens and responds in its own way.

Here are a few ways in which one can pray and communicate with the divine:

Meditative prayer: This involves focusing the mind on a particular aspect of the divine, such as a deity, and reciting prayers or mantras. This can help to clear the mind and bring a sense of peace and connection with the divine.

Contemplative prayer: This involves reflecting on the nature of the divine and one's own relationship with the divine. It can involve reading and reflecting on sacred texts, or simply sitting in silence and contemplating the divine.

Petitionary prayer: This involves making requests of the divine, such as asking for help, guidance or blessings. It can be done in a formal or informal manner and can involve reciting specific prayers or simply speaking to the divine in one's own words.

Gratitude prayer: This involves expressing gratitude to the divine for blessings and gifts received. This type of prayer can help to cultivate a sense of humility and thankfulness in the devotee.

Worship: This involves offering devotion, praise and adoration to the divine through songs, dances, rituals and other practices.

4. Chanting the Name of the Divine and Feeling the Presence

When you are in love with someone, just taking the name of the beloved can bring a thrill to you. The same magic happens when you chant the name of the divine. A common form of devotion in many spiritual traditions, repeating the name of the divine can connect one with the divine and help one experience its presence. Chanting can be done in different ways, such as by repeating the name of the divine aloud or silently, or by singing devotional songs or hymns that contain the name of the divine. The subtler the chanting, the more powerful it is—when you chant silently in your heart, it is considered many times more effective. At its subtlest, the chanting goes on continuously in the background.

There is a term called '*Ajapa Jaap*' in Sanskrit which means constant remembrance of the divine. The word 'Ajapa' means 'unstruck', referring to the sound of the mantra being repeated internally and continuously without the need for vocalization. The word 'Jaap' means 'to repeat'. In Ajapa Jaap, the mantra or the name of the divine is repeated internally, without the need for vocalization, by focusing on the sound of the breath. The breath is used as the medium for the repetition of the mantra or the name of the divine. The sound of the mantra or the name of the divine is heard internally, and it is believed that this internal repetition of the mantra or the name of the divine is more powerful than vocalized repetition. The repetition of the mantra, when weaved into the breath, becomes so inherent to us that even when we fall asleep, the mantra chanting continues as we breathe.

This practice can be done by anyone, regardless of religion or spiritual tradition. It's an easy practice to start with and it can be done at any time and anywhere, in silence or amidst noise. You can pick a mantra as simple and as profound as 'Om'. With practice and repetition, the mantra reveals its true nature of the divine.

The repetition of the mantra is believed to help focus the mind and to clear it of distractions, making it easier to connect with the divine. It is a powerful tool for building a connection with the divine and can be a way to experience the presence of the divine in one's life. Chanting becomes a very powerful form of meditation when the repetition of the mantra is used to centre oneself in the sense of 'I Am-ness' that is the door to Awareness. Chanting offers several other benefits—from gaining mystical powers to cultivating spiritual attributes such as devotion, humility and surrender to reducing feelings of stress and anxiety, and bringing a sense of inner peace and calm. The vibrations of the mantra cleanse the stored patterns imprinted in every cell of the body, replacing conditioning with the purity of the mantra. By chanting, one can experience the divine presence, and ultimately attain a state of union with the divine.

Path of Selfless Action (Karma Yoga)

Once we realize ourselves as that one pure Awareness in which myriad forms appear as the whole universe, the natural progression is to engage in selfless service. We understand fundamentally that what we do to others is what we do unto ourselves. This realization can lead to a shift in perspective, where we are motivated to engage in selfless service not out of a sense of moral duty, but out of a deep understanding of the Source of being and the interconnectedness of all things.

This understanding leads to a greater sense of compassion and empathy, and a desire to help others without expecting anything in return. This is the path of selfless action, also known as Karma Yoga, which is one of the four main paths of Yoga.

The Practice of Loving Compassion

Ignorance of life's unity fuels negative attitudes such as selfishness, envy, arrogance and a lack of compassion. This separates us from others, causing us to focus solely on our own needs at the cost of disregarding others' needs. This egoic focus drives competitive and self-centred behaviour that lacks empathy and compassion. As a result, we become unwilling to help those in need and fail to consider their well-being. The sense of separateness compels us to compete with others in order to set ourselves apart and establish our own sense of identity. This results in an insatiable desire for more, where we are never satisfied with what we have. If offered the whole earth today, the egoic insatiable greed would start demanding another planet. This constant striving for more is the source of misery and suffering, leading to feelings of dissatisfaction and unfulfilment. The mind may find ways to justify these wants, but ultimately, they can never be fully satisfied. This triggers a cycle of constant desire, where we always look for the next thing to fulfil us, but never find true satisfaction. The cycle of desire is a disease and is not recognized as such because most of us suffer from it.

Without understanding the unity of life, we also fail to recognize our connection with the natural world, leading to disregard for the environment and exploitation of resources. Knowledge of Oneness fosters a compassionate and cooperative society, where people care for each other and the environment. Serving a higher purpose fills us with fulfilment and satisfaction, as the individual self becomes a tool to spread love and joy. This is the power of putting knowledge into action.

When one is established in the knowledge of the Self, compassion for others and loving-kindness arise as natural by-products. This is because when we understand our true nature as pure Awareness, we realize that the separation between ourselves and others is a mere illusion and we are inherently connected. Being centred on the Self, the state of love is maintained, and anyone who comes into that ambit, experiences immense unconditional love. In this state, we become capable of loving unconditionally, as we are not driven by the ego's need to only want love. The love that is often considered love in today's day and age is egoic, as it is driven by the desire to possess, take and control; it is not unconditional. But the love that arises from the realization of the Self is not driven by the ego and is unconditional. This kind of love is not based on any external condition or circumstance; it is not based on what the other person does or does not do. It is a pure, selfless love that is not dependent on any external factors.

From the moment we are born, we rely heavily on the love and compassion of our mothers for survival. The love and care of a mother are essential for the physical, emotional and psychological well-being of a child. Studies have shown that infants who receive consistent, nurturing care from their mothers have better outcomes in areas such as cognitive development, mental health and overall well-being. A mother's love and compassion play a critical role in the development of a child's sense of self-worth and self-esteem. Children who experience a warm and nurturing environment at home are more likely to develop positive self-concepts, self-esteem and positive relationships with others. Furthermore, the mother's emotional support and responsiveness towards her children helps in fostering a sense of trust, security and self-worth in the children. This is how important compassion and love are in shaping our childhood.

Love and compassion are not only essential for us to survive in the early stages of life but also important for us to thrive in the later stages of life. It is through the love and support of our family, friends and community that we are able to grow and reach our full potential. The love and compassion that we received as infants should inspire us to be loving and compassionate towards others in order to help them survive and thrive.

Compassion is a fundamental aspect of human nature and is often considered to be at the core of what it means to be human. It is the ability to empathize with others, to feel their pain and suffering, and to respond with kindness and understanding. This is a key driver of pro-social behaviour and can lead to greater empathy, generosity and cooperation among individuals. It is also seen as a vital component of the emotional and moral development of human beings, as it allows us to connect with others on a deep level, and fosters feelings of kindness and understanding. Studies have shown that compassionate individuals tend to be more resilient, happier and have greater overall well-being. Compassion is a key aspect of spiritual and moral development. It is seen as a vital step in the journey towards enlightenment, or union with the divine. The cultivation of compassion can be a complete practice in itself which can lead to full enlightenment. *Bodhisattvas* practise the path of compassion and work towards benefiting all sentient beings by elevating them out of their suffering. They do this by offering the merits of their own practices for the development of all. A *Bodhisattva* takes a vow to attain enlightenment not just for their own benefit but for the benefit of all beings.

Here is the story of a young woman named Sarah, who struggled with feelings of insecurity, anxiety and self-doubt. She often found herself feeling jealous of others and constantly comparing herself to them, which only led to more feelings of inadequacy.

One day, Sarah came across a book about loving-kindness meditation and decided to give it a try. She began by focusing on phrases such as 'may I be happy, may I be healthy, may I be safe' while visualizing herself in a state of well-being. As she continued to practise, she began to notice a shift in her perspective. She started to realize that her feelings of insecurity and self-doubt were not unique to her but were something that many people struggled with. This realization led to a greater sense of compassion and empathy towards others, as she understood that they too were struggling with similar issues.

As she continued to practise, Sarah also started to notice a change in her relationships. She found that she was able to be more understanding and patient with others, and her relationships became more positive and fulfilling.

One day, Sarah had an interaction with a friend that would have normally ended in an argument. But this time, instead of getting defensive and angry, she was able to respond with compassion and understanding. This led to a deeper understanding of her friend and the relationship was strengthened.

As she continued to practise loving-kindness and compassion, Sarah began to feel a sense of inner peace and fulfilment that she had never experienced before. She realized that through this practice, she was not only helping others but was also helping herself in the process. Anything, when practised with full heart and soul, can lead us to the complete realization of truth and freedom.

Mirror neurons are a type of neurons in the brain that are thought to play a key role in empathy and social cognition. These neurons are activated both when we perform an action and when we observe the same action being performed by others. This allows us to 'mirror' the actions and emotions of others, and to understand and respond to the emotions of others. This is a mechanism by which we can 'feel' the emotions of others and empathize with their experiences. When we observe someone else experiencing joy, for example, our mirror neurons respond by simulating the experience of joy, which allows us to understand and relate to the other person's emotions. When we give others gifts and see their reaction of joy, we also receive a gift of the same joy as experienced by others because of the functioning of the mirror neurons. By giving and seeing the joy in the other person, our mirror neurons respond by simulating their experience of joy which, in turn, can lead us to experience joy as well. This is an example of how our actions can have a positive impact on both ourselves and others, as we not only bring happiness to others but also experience the same emotions.

Understanding mirror neurons can play a role in helping us follow the path of Karma Yoga or selfless action as it allows us to recognize how the emotions and experiences of others have a direct impact on us. When we observe others in need or suffering, our mirror neurons respond by simulating those experiences, which can lead to feelings of compassion and a desire to help. This can motivate us to engage in selfless service, as we understand that what we do to others, we ultimately do to ourselves. Additionally, when we engage in selfless actions, such as volunteering or helping others, we can observe the positive impact that our actions have on others, and the resulting feelings of joy, gratitude and appreciation. So, in this case, our mirror neurons respond by simulating those feelings, which lead to a sense of fulfilment. This can serve as a reinforcing mechanism, motivating us to continue to engage in selfless actions and to make helping others a regular part of our lives.

Realizing There Is No Other

As we have already understood, 'I' and 'mine' are merely mental constructs in the background of Awareness, which stays as the constant factor, and the sense of identity and permanency is due to our unreliable stored memory and the mind's tendency to create stories and narratives about ourselves and the world around us. This understanding can be constructively applied in the path of selfless action too.

Everything we know and experience is produced by our minds. We, as Awareness, are apart from the mind. The mind is full of fears and desires. It struggles to survive as it does not have an inherent existence. It borrows existence from Awareness, and because it is not real, it is always demanding our attention for its sustenance. The analogy of the moon on a new moon night is a powerful one, as it illustrates the idea of turning towards the source of light. Just as the moon on a new moon night is facing the sun, we too must turn towards the Source of our being, which is Awareness. The sun won't be lit up by the light of the moon as the sun has its own light but the moon, instead of lighting up external objects, is turned towards its source. Similarly, our minds must turn towards the Source of our being, the Awareness, instead of being externally focused and grasping the objects of the world.

To go beyond the mind, one should be silent yet alert. Silence and peace are where we realize the existence of the one—there is no other that exists in that state. Actions might appear to happen in that state but they are only observed as a play, as a movie. You remain as the screen on which this play continues to happen. In that state, the pain and pleasure of the character do not make you suffer. Only pure bliss exists, as we remain as the witnessing consciousness in a state of unconditional love. The villain and the hero are equal to us. We feel the same and equal amount of love for both. Everybody becomes worthy of our love and compassion.

Offering the Merits of Actions to the Higher Power

When the egoic self is offered at the feet of the higher Self, the individual's actions become aligned with the greater good, rather than being driven by personal desires or aspirations. All activities are seen as the play and will of the higher Self. The individual realizes that there is no separate 'I' to claim the merits of the actions as everything is done according to the divine will. This realization switches perspective, and the individual starts to see themselves as an instrument of the higher power, rather than as the doer of their actions. A greater sense of humility, detachment from the fruits of one's actions and a deeper understanding of the interconnectedness of all things are born from this knowledge. The heart is filled with compassion and empathy towards others, as the individual understands that their actions are not for personal gain, but for the benefit of all.

Giving up the Assumption of Doership

There have been several scientific studies and experiments that have attempted to provide evidence for the idea that we are not the doers of our actions. One such study is the Libet experiment, which was conducted by neuroscientist Benjamin Libet in the 1980s. In the experiment, participants were asked to perform a simple action, such as raising their hands, while their brain activity was being monitored. The results showed that there was a noticeable change in brain activity (a so-called 'readiness potential') before the participants were consciously aware of making the decision to move their hands. This suggests that the brain was preparing for the action before the participant was conscious of making the decision to move their hand, supporting the idea that the action happens first, and then the sense of 'I' comes and claims it.

Another study that is relevant is the experiments on the free will illusion, which has been conducted by various neuroscientists and philosophers. These studies have shown that the sense of control and agency that we experience when we perform an action is an illusion created by the brain and that our actions are actually determined by a complex set of neural processes that occur before we are even aware of them.

As long as we desire to influence events, liberation is not for us. The notion of doership is the cause of all of our bondage.

As long as we think we are the character we are playing, the circumstances and the predicaments of the character will deeply influence us. We will desire good things for the character and fear bad things happening to the character. We will replay our habits and feel stuck. To change our ways, we need to examine these habitual feelings and tendencies closely. We are in bondage because of inattentiveness. The solution is to be attentive to thought patterns every moment and then gently bring attention to the Awareness, which is the witness consciousness to all thoughts.

We have to realize that all comes from within. The world we experience is the projection of our own mind. Just as we project our dream world, this world is no different. The external world is not separate from us but a reflection of our own thoughts and beliefs. But when we identify ourselves with the body, mind and character, we become trapped in the egoic self, and we become attached to our thoughts and beliefs. This attachment can lead to a sense of separation and disconnection from others. It can also lead to a sense of conflict and division. The identification with certain ideas can even become compulsive and lead to religious or any other fanaticism, where individuals are willing to fight and even kill others in the defence of their own set of beliefs. This is all a result of the identification with the egoic self and the belief that our own beliefs are the only true ones.

All these different paths are not separate ways of attaining Self-realization—they are all related and dependent on each other.

4

Stabilizing as the Awareness and Living Enlightenment

'Enlightenment is not a state, it is a process. The process of freeing ourselves from our limitations, from our attachments, from our habits and conditioning, from our suffering.'—*Jiddu Krishnamurti*

Having experienced a breakthrough and a moment of pure Awareness, the next step is to stabilize and maintain this state as in *sahaja* samadhi (a state of effortless, natural, spontaneous Awareness). To do so, we can employ two modes of cultivation. The first is to actively disassociate from the mind, recognizing when it tries to pull us away from the present moment and redirecting our attention back to the pure Awareness. The second mode is to recognize that the mind is also a projection in the Awareness and is not separate from us, allowing us to embrace its activity with a sense of detachment and observe its workings from a place of stillness. The nature of Awareness is one of unconditional acceptance and openness, welcoming whatever arises without resistance or craving. It is in this space of pure Awareness that we can find peace and freedom from the limitations of the mind. By cultivating a practice of dissociation and recognition, we can more easily stabilize in this state of sahaja samadhi, experiencing the fullness of life with clarity and presence.

In this chapter, we will explore in detail these two modes of cultivation that can aid us in stabilizing in the pure Awareness and living as enlightened beings. As we previously mentioned, the first mode involves disassociating from our habitual mental patterns or we can aptly label it as 'unplugging from the robot mode'.

The second mode of cultivation involves letting go of all effort and relaxing in and as the pure Awareness. The Awareness is not only limited to the subject or witness consciousness but also includes the objective world that is manifested. This understanding helps us to see that there is nothing separate from the Awareness, and the appearance of the world is an aspect of the Awareness itself. This world of appearances borrows its existence from Awareness and cannot exist without it. While we may exist separately from the world, such as in deep sleep or a samadhi state, the world cannot exist apart from the witnessing consciousness of the 'I'. Therefore, the world is nothing but 'I', and it has no independent existence. With this understanding, we do not resist or become enemies of the world. Instead, we see it as an expression of our own glory, and all our sufferings melt away as we recognize that the world is not separate from us.

The First Mode of Cultivation of Pure Awareness

Mental Purification: Dissociation from accumulated mental patterns and tendencies

Despite having a breakthrough and understanding non-duality, our minds might raise questions: *Why do I not experience a sense of unity and oneness? Why do I still feel like a separate self and not see everything as arising within me? Additionally, why am I still prone to emotions like passion and anger? When I encounter something I desire, I feel a strong urge to possess it. When I face insults, I experience anger and hatred. When I receive praise, I feel elated and appreciated. I constantly judge others based on their appearance and behaviour, categorizing them as attractive, unattractive, intelligent or unintelligent. In spite of all my knowledge, why do I struggle to experience myself as Awareness?*

We have to recognize that the mind and emotions are not problems to be solved, but rather aspects of our being that can be observed and understood. When we experience feelings of passion, anger and other strong emotions, we should try to observe them without getting caught up in them. We should see them as objects arising in Awareness, and not identify with them. Over time, this practice can help us develop greater detachment from our emotions and thoughts.

Until the understanding of non-duality becomes a tangible and integral part of our lives, we will feel trapped in the cycle of habitual thoughts and emotions. Even though we may gain insight into our true nature, it is only through consistent practice and embedding that knowledge in every cell of our body that we fully realize and live the peace and bliss of pure Awareness. This requires a process of stabilizing in our pure nature of witnessing Awareness and incorporating it into our daily lives.

During the stabilization phase, everyday life becomes a working pad to test one's understanding. For example, if a friend were to shout at us, we would observe the shouting as happening to a body-mind complex within us, rather than reacting personally. Our identification with the body-mind would have diminished to the point where there is no longer an emotional response to external stimuli or provocations. If there is a need to communicate something of significance, it is done in an objective manner without a trace of self-seeking. Even the loss of a loved one, which is a very painful experience, can be overcome with the strength and insight gained from this knowledge. Over time, the challenges of the individual self no longer have a significant impact on the witnessing Awareness that we are.

Let us consider another example: Suppose you find yourself in an unfortunate circumstance where your superior at work not only takes credit for your work but also berates and insults you. Your visceral response might be agitation and an intense desire to lash back at your thankless boss. However, instead of acting on your impulses, you can take a different approach involving two steps. First, observe the triggered reaction, such as palpitation, shortness of breath, heat, sweat and the compulsive desire to react aggressively. Second, become aware of the Awareness itself in which the reaction is taking place. It's important to note that suppressing your reaction is different from observing it. Suppressing reactions leads to accumulating more trauma, whereas observing reactions separates you from them and liberates you from psychically storing them as new impressions. Becoming aware of the Awareness helps you to break the cycle of identification with the character.

If we are not our minds, then why is the purification of the mind an essential step?

Purification of the mind is an essential step on the spiritual journey because it can help us completely dissolve the illusory sense of self that is created by the mind. While we are not the mind, the impurities in the mind can create an attachment to the false self, leading us to identify with our thoughts, emotions and behaviours. The impure mind can be compared to a muddy pond that is unable to reflect the clear sky. The mud in the pond represents the impurities in the mind, and as long as they remain, the mind is unable to reflect the true nature of reality. Purification of the mind is like clearing the mud from the pond, allowing the mind to become clear and reflective. Furthermore, as the mind becomes purer, it becomes easier to access the Awareness that is beyond the mind.

The force of accumulated thought patterns and tendencies (Samskaras)

'All people, wise or not, act according to the nature they have acquired through lifetimes of conditioning. Then what can repression accomplish?'—Krishna

In this quote, Sri Krishna acknowledges that our accumulated thought patterns and tendencies can strongly influence our actions. These impressions are formed through our past experiences, actions and even ancestral karma, and they can become deeply ingrained in our psyche, influencing our behaviour, without us even realizing it. From tendencies of lust and anger to pride and jealousy, these traits are inherent to human nature, and even the wisest of us are not immune to their influence. Deeply engraved, these tendencies are rooted in our subconscious mind and can be compared to a river with strong currents. Overcoming them requires significant effort, and failure to do so could result in being easily swept away by their influence. Ignoring or repressing them is not an effective solution.

Consider these inherent tendencies (samskaras) as pathways in the brain that are strengthened through repetition. Similar to how a well-trodden path in a forest is easier to follow than a new one, the neural pathways in our brains become stronger and more automatic the more we repeat certain actions or behaviours. If someone consistently practises positive behaviours such as kindness and generosity, their brain is more likely to form positive samskaras, making it easier for them to continue those actions in the future. Conversely, if someone engages in harmful or negative behaviours, their brain is more likely to form negative samskaras, making it harder to break those habits.

Addiction serves as a prime example of a powerful negative samskara. Repeatedly engaging in a behaviour of substance consumption creates strong neural pathways in the brain, which reinforce the behaviour and make it increasingly difficult to resist. Over time, the brain becomes conditioned to associate the behaviour or substance with pleasure, making it nearly impossible to break the habit. Even after a person stops engaging in the behaviour or consuming the substance, the negative samskaras associated with addiction can persist, leading to a high likelihood of relapse.

Harnessing the Kali—the Subconscious Mind

Our conscious mind includes our thoughts, feelings and sensations, as well as our ability to reason, make decisions and solve problems. It is estimated that our conscious mind makes up about 5–10 per cent of our mental activity. The subconscious mind, on the other hand, includes all the mental processes that occur outside our consciousness, such as automatic thoughts, emotions and behaviours, as well as the habits and patterns of thought that we may not be aware of. The subconscious may be estimated to make up to 95 per cent or more of our mental activity.

While we are not usually aware of our subconscious processes, they can have a significant impact on our thoughts, feelings and actions. For example, if we have a deep-seated fear of public speaking, our subconscious mind may cause us to feel anxious and nervous whenever we are asked to give a speech, even if we consciously want to do it.

Similarly, our subconscious mind can influence our beliefs, attitudes and values, shaping our perception of the world around us. If we have deeply ingrained negative beliefs about ourselves, such as 'I am not good enough', our subconscious mind may cause us to doubt ourselves and our abilities, even if we consciously know that these beliefs are not valid.

Harnessing the subconscious mind, called 'Kali' in Sanskrit, can be a challenging task as the greater part of our mind operates on a subconscious level. To train the subconscious mind, we must first become aware of the negative patterns and tendencies that we wish to overcome. This requires introspection and self-reflection, as well as a willingness to be honest with ourselves about our own limitations and weaknesses.

As the fifth girl child in my family, my arrival was met with tears by my grandmothers instead of the usual rejoicing. My parents had been hoping for a son and continued having children in pursuit of that dream. As I grew up, I noticed that my mother had a special affection for my little brother, despite her attempts to love us all equally. I often watched as she, overflowing with love, shared food from her plate with him. We were just a year apart in age, and while I longed for the same warmth and affection, my mother's love for my brother seemed to come effortlessly. This experience left me with a deep yearning for unconditional love.

To this day, this subconscious need for unconditional love and acceptance still lingers within me, but I have found solace in a valuable lesson imparted by my mother. As a child, my mother told me that while people may come and go, God will always be there to love and care for me, to listen to me and guide me. From that point on, God became my closest confidant. I would pour out my heart to Him, and He would respond with guidance and support. He became my rock, my father, my mother, my best friend and my everything. Despite facing many obstacles, I never broke down because I knew He was with me, stronger than any problem I faced. My faith in Him only grew stronger with time. I don't know if I have fully overcome my need to be loved unconditionally and maybe it's strong conditioning, but the love of God has brought me profound healing and comfort.

Pure Mind and Pure Awareness are Not Different

The process of purifying the mind involves eliminating negative thoughts, emotions and tendencies and replacing them with positive ones that are in alignment with our true nature as Awareness. Even though Awareness is pure and beyond all qualities, by purifying our mind and removing the impurities that cloud our perception, we can align ourselves with our higher Self and manifest our divine nature. This process leads to the emergence of qualities like compassion and kindness, which are expressions of the love and goodness that permeate all existence.

As Awareness, we are all-encompassing, and this aspect naturally gives rise to loving-kindness and compassion. When we realize that we are not separate from others, we naturally want to help alleviate their suffering and promote their well-being.

Again, as Awareness, we are eternally detached and do not cling to anything that arises within us. This recognition that all objects of desire are impermanent and transitory allows us to avoid becoming attached to or being controlled by them in the same way as the ego-mind. This detachment also allows us to be free from the negative emotions of lust, greed and jealousy, which are based on the illusion of separateness and the desire to possess or control. Instead, we can appreciate the beauty and impermanence of all things, without becoming attached or averse to them, as we recognize that they are simply a distorted manifestation of our true nature.

In essence, cultivating positive qualities is not about acquiring something new but about uncovering and revealing the natural qualities that are already present within us. As we align ourselves with our true nature, we realize that morality is not merely a set of rules to avoid punishment or seek rewards but an integral expression of our true nature as Awareness.

How do we break the chain of our inherent negative tendencies?

Breaking the chain of negative tendencies or samskaras is not an easy task, but it is possible with practice and discipline. We must approach and encounter our samskaras with Awareness. We must work deliberately to replace them with insights and positive reinforcement.

Here are practices and techniques we must follow to gradually develop the ability to not react impulsively when triggered by strong likes and dislikes:

Mindfulness: Becoming more aware of our thoughts, emotions and behaviours is the first step towards breaking the chain of samskaras. Through self-reflection, we become more aware of our unconscious patterns and tendencies.

Self-control: Once we become aware of our tendencies, we can begin to exercise self-control over our thoughts and behaviours. This requires a great deal of practice and discipline as we must learn to resist the pull of our conditioned tendencies and choose a different course of action.

Positive action: By consciously choosing positive actions and behaviours, we can begin to build new positive tendencies that support our growth and well-being. For example, by cultivating qualities such as kindness, generosity and compassion, we can gradually replace negative tendencies such as anger, selfishness and jealousy. The process can also be looked at as rewiring our neural pathways.

Spiritual practices: Practices such as meditation, prayer and selfless service help break the chain of negative tendencies and cultivate positive qualities. These practices help purify the mind and create a more positive and peaceful inner environment, which in turn supports positive actions and behaviours.

There is a story of a Buddhist monk who embarked on a journey of inner transformation. He sat in meditation for hours, every day, under the guidance of his wise teacher. One day, the teacher gave him a bowl and instructed him to collect black stones and white stones. 'Every time a negative thought enters your mind during meditation, place a black stone in the bowl. And every time a positive thought arises, place a white stone in the bowl,' said the teacher.

In the beginning, the monk found that his mind was plagued by negative thoughts. Black stones piled up in the bowl, while white stones were few and far between. But the monk persevered, determined to master his mind.

As the months went by, the monk noticed a shift in the balance of stones. Due to his vigilance, he was getting better at recognizing negative thoughts and replacing them with positive ones. The traffic policeman in his mind was working tirelessly, cutting off the negative thoughts and directing the flow towards positive ones. Over time, he found that he was putting more and more white stones in the bowl, and fewer black ones. After a year or two of consistent practice, he found that the bowl was filled mostly with white stones and very few black ones. The monk had succeeded in purifying his subconscious mind, and the job of meditation became easier. The monk's journey of self-discovery and transformation came to a beautiful fruition, leaving him with a heart full of love and a mind full of clarity.

The process of breaking negative conditioning of the mind can be aided by practising positive ones and ultimately transcending the negative patterns through self-knowledge. However, it is not an easy task, as negative patterns can be dense and heavy, and our mind can easily get caught up in likes and dislikes, which hold us back and keep us tied to our ego. Dislikes, in particular, can be our biggest enemy, creating feelings of fear and insecurity that prevent us from experiencing true vibrancy, happiness and joy. When we are able to move beyond our likes and dislikes, we enter into a state of bliss. Everyone is divine, but our likes and dislikes act as a shell that obscures our true nature. The thicker the shell, the more we suffer. Our likes should also not turn into cravings, as this can limit our potential and be heavily binding.

Imagine your mind as a garden, filled with all kinds of plants and flowers. Some of these are beautiful, fragrant and healthy, while others are withered, prickly and diseased. Just like a garden, our minds need tending, care and attention. And just like a garden, we can remove the weeds and cultivate the flowers to create a more beautiful and vibrant space.

Breaking the negative conditioning of the mind is like pulling out the weeds from your garden. It's not an easy task, but with patience and practice, it's possible. Practising positive tendencies is like planting new seeds in your garden. By watering and nurturing these seeds, you can create a new positive pattern in your mind.

As one continues to cultivate positive tendencies, the mind becomes more refined and open, paving the way for the revelation of self-knowledge. Self-knowledge can only dawn in a positive or *sattvic* mind. Positive or sattvic tendencies are closer to our nature as awareness and hence are not binding. The purity and clarity of such a mind allow for a deeper understanding of one's true nature and the realization of the ultimate reality.

Tricks of the Mind

A closer observation of the mind reveals that it never truly ceases. Our minds are constantly engaged in an internal dialogue, shaped by the conditioning we have experienced throughout our lives. This internal voice is incessant, and even if we have experienced a breakthrough, it continues. However, we can focus on transforming this dialogue into something pure and enlightened, in line with a sattvic mindset. A pure mind has the ability to avoid getting entangled in this dialogue and instead remain aware of its presence. To illustrate this, let us consider a conversation between a mind that is still attached to personal identity and a mind that has transcended it.

Here is a dialogue between a conditioned mind that is suffering from negativity (identified mind) and a fully purified mind (free mind):

The identified mind: 'I can't believe I have so much to do today. I don't even know where to start. Maybe I should make a to-do list. No, that's a waste of time. I should just get started on something. But what should I do first? Maybe I should check my email. Oh no, I just remembered that I have a meeting in an hour. I'd better start getting ready for that. Wait, what am I going to wear? I should probably pick out my clothes now. But I don't have anything clean. I need to do the laundry. Ugh, when am I ever going to have time for all of this?'

The free mind: 'There is a lot to do today, but that's okay. I will take things one at a time and stay present in the moment. I can make a plan, but I don't need to get too attached to it. I will be flexible and open to whatever comes up. I am not my to-do list, and my worth does not depend on how much I accomplish. I am just here, in this moment, breathing and alive.'

As you can see, the identified mind is caught up in its own thoughts and worries, while the free mind is able to observe those thoughts without getting stuck in them. The free mind is more present and aware and is able to respond to the situation with calmness and clarity.

Identified mind: 'I'm so stressed out right now. I have so many deadlines coming up, and I don't think I'll be able to get everything done in time. What if I fail? What will people think of me?'

Free mind: 'Yes, there is a lot on my plate right now, but I can only do what I can do. I will focus on one thing at a time, and trust that I'll be able to handle whatever comes my way. My worth is not dependent on my productivity or success, and I don't need to worry about what others think of me.'

Identified mind: 'I'm so angry at my friend for cancelling on me at the last minute. I can't believe they would do that to me. I should just stop talking to them altogether.'

Free mind: 'I feel disappointed that my friend cancelled on me, but I don't need to take it personally. Maybe they're dealing with something difficult and couldn't make it. I'll reach out to them and see if there's anything I can do to support them.'

Identified mind: 'I'm so anxious about this presentation I have to give. What if I forget what I'm supposed to say? What if everyone thinks I'm a terrible speaker?'

Free mind: 'I'm feeling some nerves about this presentation, but that's normal. I've prepared as much as I can, and I trust that I'll be able to handle any curveballs that come my way. Even if I make a mistake, it's not the end of the world. I'll take some deep breaths and focus on being present in the moment.'

In each of these examples, the identified mind is caught up in negative thoughts and emotions, while the free or sattvic mind is able to observe those thoughts without getting stuck in them. The free mind is more centred, calm and compassionate, and is able to respond to situations in a way that is more aligned with higher values and aspirations.

As we have observed, a pure mind has the ability to avoid getting trapped in thought patterns and instead remains present in the moment with a heightened focus. However, there are instances when life presents us with deeply challenging circumstances, such as losing a loved one or facing a serious illness. In such situations, it can be difficult to maintain a positive outlook. Let us consider how the dialogue might go when we encounter such difficult circumstances in our lives.

Identified mind: 'I can't believe they're gone. I'll never be able to see or talk to them again. How can I go on without them? Everything feels so meaningless now.'

Free mind: 'I feel a deep sense of loss, but I know that they will always be with me in some way. I can honour their memory by living my life in a way that would make them proud. It's okay to grieve and feel the pain, but I don't need to get stuck in it forever.'

Identified mind: 'Will I ever be able to come out of the grief and find peace? What if I never come out of this pain?'

Free mind: 'Grief is a natural response to loss, and it's important to allow ourselves to feel the pain and sadness that comes with it. But we don't have to stay trapped in our grief. Instead, we can use our pain as an opportunity to grow and find deeper meaning in our lives. These situations can be looked upon as a wake-up call from the divine. We have to wake up to our real selves as Awareness. When we identify with the person who is experiencing the loss, the grief becomes intense and overwhelming. However, when we recognize that the person and the experience are just appearances in consciousness, the identification with the person dissolves and the grip of the grief loosens. We come to understand that the person who has died is not truly gone, they have just taken on a different form. The experience of loss is just a movement in consciousness, and like all movements, it will eventually pass. The peace that we seek is not something that can be found in external circumstances, it is already present within us, waiting to be recognized. When we rest in the stillness of Awareness, even in the midst of loss and grief, we begin to experience a deep and abiding peace that is not dependent on external circumstances.'

Identified mind: 'Is it truly possible to be untouched by pain? Anything can happen tomorrow. I can lose all my wealth and health.'

Free mind: 'The idea that we can be completely untouched by pain is a misconception. Pain is a natural part of life, and it's unrealistic to expect to be immune from it. However, it's possible to find a sense of peace and equanimity in the midst of difficult experiences. Inner peace doesn't come from trying to control or avoid pain, but from connecting with the deeper Awareness that is beyond the fluctuating thoughts and emotions of the mind. This Awareness that we are is always present, even amidst the pain and suffering, and can provide a sense of stability and security. By connecting to the Source, the Awareness, we can develop a resilient mind and heart that can help us navigate the ups and downs of life with grace and ease.'

Identified mind: 'But what about practicality? How can we live our lives without the fear of pain and loss?'

Free mind: 'When we are able to recognize the impermanence of all things and let go of our attachment to external circumstances, we can begin to live in a state of freedom. We will still experience pain and loss, but they will no longer have the power to grip and control us. We will understand that everything is transitory and that this too shall pass. In this understanding, we can find peace and contentment in the present moment, no matter what the external circumstances may be. This is not a denial of the reality of pain and loss, but a recognition that they are not the ultimate truth of who we are. Our true nature is not the person who is suffering, but the Awareness that is witnessing the experience. By recognizing this, we can begin to live our lives with a sense of ease and grace, even in the face of challenges and difficulties.'

Identified mind: 'How to connect to the Source?'

Free mind: 'You are the Source, the Awareness. You are not the mind. When the sense of 'I am-ness' frees itself from identification with the physical and mental selves, it becomes truly enlightened. The identification with the body and mind creates the illusion of separation and insecurity. It is this illusion of separation that causes us to experience pain and suffering. When we feel ourselves to be the limited self, we desire, we want, we crave. Observe that what you are is changeless. Thoughts come and go. Something that was so important to us in the past, for the fulfilment of which you remained restless for days together, what is its value now? Even if you achieved it, is your mind truly peaceful now?'

Identified mind: 'Can we ever find true peace of mind?'

Free mind: 'The mind causes insecurity so that it can stay in charge. It makes us imagine situations where we feel weak and out of control. Imagining these situations fills us with fear and restlessness. The other name for the mind is restlessness. We can try all sorts of ways to bring peace to the mind, but any peace-of-mind experience is not long-lasting; it is ephemeral. We can get into a thoughtless state for a moment or two but then the restlessness starts again. If we examine closely, we observe that the mind has constant simmering thoughts in the background. The restless mind operates by chasing pleasure and avoiding pain. What we think is progress is a pleasant state of mind over an unpleasant one. These fluctuations in the mind cannot bring us to the ultimate liberation.'

Real peace of mind comes by completely disconnecting from the mind. The Awareness is peace itself; it does not need to borrow peace from the flickering mind. We are ever liberated; we need not keep begging the mind to provide us with peace. It can never do that because it is not capable of doing that. Peace shines through and causes gaps in the incessant chattering of the mind. Thoughts are movements and therefore restless; Awareness is stillness and is therefore peace.

Identified mind: 'Relationships give us joy and bring us fulfilment. We believe that if only we can find the love of our lives, can we stay truly happy.'

Free mind: 'Expecting a relationship to be the solution to all our problems is a delusion. We are expecting an event in time to resolve all our problems. Has that ever happened? Has any event in time brought us eternal peace? Expecting a relationship to make us happy is a trap that our minds easily fall into, that once we find the love of our lives, all will be well. But in reality, this is not the case. Our mind always promises us fulfilment in the near future, never in the here and now; this is the trick of the mind. It always tells us that happiness is right there at the next turn. If we fulfil just this desire and get rid of just this fear, that's it, we will be happy then—these are the illusions created by the mind to keep us hankering for illusive joy in externalities. While relationships can bring happiness and fulfilment, they are not immune to challenges and disappointments. It's important to cultivate happiness independently and not solely rely on a relationship to provide it.

A Sattvic Mind and the Practice of Self-Awareness

According to Tulku Urgyen Rinpoche, once we have truly received the pointing-out instructions and recognize the mind essence, becoming fully realized through training is not out of reach. It is in your own hands. As the mind is purified, focus deepens, paving the way for even greater breakthroughs. This process is cyclical, with each level of purification leading to a higher level of focus which in turn leads to an even deeper level of breakthroughs. Imagine a pole being driven into the ground: with each push, it sinks deeper and deeper, gradually reaching new depths.

With the purification of the mind, the practice of self-awareness gets easier. The ultimate aim is to transcend the identification with the mind altogether and recognize the Source of the mind, which is pure Awareness. Breakthroughs enable us to uncover the limitless potential that lies within us.

While knowledge and insight are important, they are not enough to experience divine joy and romance in every moment. For that, we must continuously practise staying with the insight or knowledge, choosing Awareness over the thoughts in the mind. Practising the art of happiness requires effort, just like any other skill. Every time we come back to Awareness and negate our thoughts, we are building our self-awareness muscle. Just as any art practised for many hours gets refined and brings joy, recognizing that we are Awareness and returning to it with effort becomes easier with time. As a result, the remembrance becomes effortless, and the joy becomes boundless.

When we are centred in our Awareness, we start to live our enlightenment. In this state, we are free from suffering and experience the highest bliss, which is not dependent on external circumstances.

Why is it necessary to practise the art of Awareness at every moment?

We have practised being the body, mind and character for time immemorial and therefore our habit patterns are formed accordingly. As long as we have the body, the habit patterns are deeply engraved in us. We will experience pain and pleasure through the senses and the mind. Insight gained from a spiritual breakthrough is not sufficient on its own. To ensure that the habit patterns of the mind and body do not have a deep impact on us, we must engage in regular practice. Think of it this way—just as we need to exercise regularly to maintain physical fitness, we also need to practise the art of Awareness regularly to maintain mental and spiritual fitness. Without regular practice, our minds will keep defaulting to the old habit patterns and we will continue to be stuck in our limited sense of self.

When we fully understand and accept that our true nature is Awareness, it becomes easier to play the character we've come to play in the world. We can effortlessly embody the roles we choose to take on, whether a mother, sister, daughter or any other role. By viewing ourselves as actors playing a role, we can experience the emotions and play our roles convincingly. We can let go of the attachment to the limited sense of self and freely express the divine qualities that we choose to embody in our 'role'. It also helps us to not get caught up in the ego-driven dramas that can arise in daily life, as we remember that these are just part of the play and not our true nature. As we project the world of our dreams during the dream state, similarly, this world too is the projection of our own mind. An understanding like this helps us to enjoy the play thoroughly with a greater sense of detachment and freedom.

A deep transformation occurs when the intellect is focused on exploring the essence of being. All the personal egocentric desires fall off and the intellect becomes more refined and skilful in seeing through the projections of names, forms and functions. This leads to a deeper understanding and stabilization in and as the Awareness, which is the light behind the play in which the play is happening and is being known.

By bringing our attention back to the Awareness, we are working to counteract the habit patterns of identifying with the individual self and the body-mind complex. This shift in focus can lead to the emergence of pure habit patterns, as our intellect is no longer seeking worldly pleasures and has found peace in staying with the true essence of our being. The goal is to cultivate this habit of staying with the Awareness and to gradually let go of the habit patterns of identifying with the limited self. By the sheer power of practice, our intellect reaches a state where even while engaged in daily activities our mind is resting in Awareness. It is as if our attention has been split in two directions—one towards the work we are doing, like cooking, walking and so on, and the other towards the sense of 'I Am-ness'. This allows us to live in the world, while also maintaining a connection to our true nature. With continued practice, the background of pure Awareness becomes more prominent and pronounced.

Have you ever eaten something sweet and enjoyed the pleasant sensations it brings to your tongue and mind? That's the physical experience. But with a refined intellect, you can see beyond the sensory experience and grasp the true nature of pure Awareness. This kind of refined intellect uses every situation as an opportunity to continuously experience the Self. It's like an X-ray beam that goes directly to the bone without being distracted by the flesh. A wise person recognizes the Awareness in everything, without being distracted by the passing waves of experiences. With practice, the continuously changing world becomes the nature and projection of the Self. Every bit of this play, every character, every situation appears as magic created by the Self.

And as you cultivate this Awareness, you begin to feel a true sense of oneness with everything. You see the ocean of Awareness, rather than getting lost in the waves of appearances.

During a Vipassana retreat I attended, I honed my ability to focus on the sensations in my body for extended periods of time during meditation. Whenever pain arose, I was able to maintain a state of equanimity and observe the sensation objectively instead of reacting with aversion. Instead of automatically reacting to pain with movement, I was able to use my razor-sharp mind to zoom in on the area of pain and observe the sensations of pain as nothing but a constant rise and fall of vibrations. My mind observed objectively and remained steadfast in its equanimity, without labelling the sensations as pain. Over the course of the ten-day retreat, I went without sleep for eight nights as my mind constantly reminded me to keep observing the sensations in my body. I had gladly become a sensation-seeker, but definitely a wise one. Once during the night, I even experienced a deep blue-purple light while lying in bed with my eyes closed. Despite the extraordinary appearance, my practice of equanimity enabled me to simply observe the light without getting carried away by the excitement. This experience solidified my understanding that no matter what appears outside of us, we can choose to remain equanimous and avoid being swayed by cravings or aversions.

The Imposter Self

Picture yourself walking through a bustling city street, with a sea of people rushing past you, each lost in their own world. Amidst the chaos, you suddenly become aware that everyone around you is plagued by the attachment to their individual identities. They are trapped in the same cycle of suffering.

This attachment to personhood is akin to a virus that infects us all, but it's so deeply ingrained in us that we don't even recognize it as a problem. Like a stealthy thief, it gradually steals away our joy, leaving us feeling empty and disconnected.

Everything we strive to hold on to as individuals—youth, vitality, wealth, possessions—inevitably slips through our fingers, leaving us with a sense of sorrow and loss. First, we work hard to acquire things, then we work harder to maintain them, and ultimately feel heartache when we lose them. The natural order of things is that they appear, linger for a while, and eventually disappear. If we wish to escape from the suffering caused by this cycle of attachment and loss, we must relinquish the habits and addictions that lead us to cling to transitory things. While material possessions may provide fleeting pleasure, we must ask ourselves: *who is the enjoyer, the one experiencing this enjoyment?* The sensations we feel come and go, and their very impermanence is what makes them perceptible. If sensations were permanent or continuous, we would not be able to distinguish one sensation from another. It is the perception of change that brings us closer to the changeless backdrop of our existence, the Awareness that is constant amidst continuous change.

One could argue that our very own existence is the cause of all our suffering. It is the person we imagine ourselves as, who suffers with its storyline, memories and habits. Our true Self, the pure Awareness that lies beyond the limitations of the ego, is ever liberated.

To reach our highest Self, we must reject all that we can identify as 'this'. The path of '*Neti-Neti*' ('not this, not that' in Sanskrit) is the only effective way to achieve this. In this practice, we examine all aspects of our identity, including our thoughts, emotions, physical sensations and perceptions, and we systematically reject each one as 'not the self'. By doing so, we strip away all layers of false identity until we are left with only the pure essence of our being, which is our highest Self. In the end, what we truly are can never be denied, and it will always remain with us. It's only the false ideas we have about ourselves that we must let go of. Both faith and logic teach us that we are not the body or its desires and fears, nor are we the mind and its imagined concepts, nor the persona we play in the world. Our task is simply to relinquish the false, and the truth will reveal itself. The mind can only know what is within the mind, but our true essence is Awareness, which transcends the mind.

How do we know something which is beyond the mind? Will it always remain unknown?

Insight reveals that we know ourselves before we know anything else outside us, because nothing can exist without us being there to experience its existence. Therefore, our own existence is a prior and necessary factor before the existence of anything else. We imagine we do not know ourselves because we cannot define ourselves, but can we ever exclaim 'I am not'? Even if we do, we exist as the one who is denying the existence of oneself. We can only know ourselves by being ourselves. There is nothing out there to be grasped.

Once we understand that anything perceived cannot be the perceiver, we can apply ourselves to let go of all our false identifications. The ego-self creates a false sense of self as the protagonist, drawing on elements of self-consciousness from pure Awareness and constructing a narrative based on transient thoughts and emotions.

The imposter self or the ego is an illusion that arises due to our attachment to thoughts and desires. It is bound by self-created desires and fears, and suffers from the memories and expectations it has created for itself. Abandoning memories and expectations is the best way to get rid of this false sense of self. The imposter self deceives us into thinking that the next achievement or possession will bring us lasting happiness and peace. We constantly chase after material possessions, educational degrees, romantic relationships, marriage and children, but none of these things can provide us with true fulfilment. We are stuck in a never-ending cycle, and before we know it, we are at the end of our lives. This feeling of incompleteness is what drives us throughout our lives, and it is all due to the illusion created by the imposter self. With the dissolution of the 'I', personal suffering disappears.

The Illusion of Doership Created by the Imposter Self

The imposter self deceives us into believing that we are the ones in control, but in reality, everything is happening to us and nothing is done by us. Our desires and their fulfilment are impulses planted by nature, and we have no real power over them.

Just as a cinema screen is simply a canvas for images to be projected with no inherent control over the projected movie, we are the canvas upon which life unfolds. We are not the images or forms that appear on the screen, but rather the screen itself, and we appear to be one with the projection. Even if a fire burns down an entire city in a movie, it does not affect the actual screen. Similarly, the events of life cannot harm our true essence as the screen of Awareness. This is what happens in our dreams too, where we may be chased by lions or fly through the air, but remain safe and untouched in our waking lives. We have always been untouched Awareness, separate from all appearances yet permeating all of them.

The realization that everything is predetermined and beyond our control can be liberating. It allows us to release ourselves from the burdensome weight of worry and anxiety that stems from trying to manipulate outcomes. The idea of being a doer, with all its associated feelings of guilt and pride, can be discarded. We can simply observe life unfolding without getting attached to any particular outcome. By relinquishing control and surrendering to the flow of life, we can finally break free from the shackles of desires and fears created by the imposter self.

At this point, we may question the desire for freedom itself, wondering if it is simply another trick played by the imposter self. However, the desire for self-liberation is different from the illusion created by the imposter self. This desire is part of the *Vidyamaya* (the aspect of illusion which leads to self-knowledge) and helps us burn away all our desires until we are left with nothing but pure Awareness.

Ramana Maharshi used the analogy of a burning stick to explain this concept. To set a log of wood on fire, you need a burning stick. Once the wood is burnt, the stick is thrown away with the rest of the burning wood. Similarly, Vidyamaya helps us burn away all our desires, and once this process is complete, it, too, is destroyed.

The False Notion of 'I' and 'Mine' Created by the Imposter Self

The false idea of 'I' and 'mine' is another trap that the imposter self uses to keep us enchained. We develop attachments to the people we cherish and the things we possess, but the truth is that they possess us instead. We become bound by the very things we are attached to. For instance, if our home were to be destroyed by an earthquake today, we would experience an immense sense of loss, but we wouldn't feel the same pain if it were someone else's home. Our possessions exercise control over us. Similarly, when we lose someone we love, the pain can be excruciating, but if a stranger were to die, it would hardly impact us. Therefore, it's not the person themselves that is important, but our attachment to them.

We cling tightly to the people and things we possess because we fear losing them and the pain they would cause us. But have we ever stopped to ponder why? Holding on to people and things gives us a sense of expansion and feeds the imposter self.

However, does this mean that we can never truly love someone? We can, but when we unconditionally love someone, we don't bind or possess them. In short, we aren't attached to them. Even if they were to pass away, though we would grieve, we would also recognize that only their physical body has departed and their soul continues its journey.

The concepts of 'me' and 'mine' are mere illusions that limit our understanding of reality. For true reality to manifest, we must relinquish our attachment to these limiting notions. Clinging tightly to these ideas only keeps us trapped. Our true nature as Awareness is one of detachment. Every night, we let go of our storylines, our worries and our loved ones, as we drift off to sleep. We recognize on some level that these attachments are not necessary for our survival or happiness. Even a mother who loves her newborn deeply can find peace in letting go and falling asleep. Our natural state is not defined by our bodies or minds, nor by the concepts of 'I' or 'mine'. It is a state of pure being, free from any labels or attachments.

Portals into the State of Enlightenment

Holding on to 'I Am'

How do we define reality? What is the ultimate gauge to find out if something is real? For something to be considered real, it must be permanent, existing infinitely and eternally. But what is the one thing in our lives that meets this criterion? Take a moment to reflect before answering.

As you ponder this, you will start to think about the things in your life that have stayed permanent. Maybe you will think about your relationships, your possessions or your accomplishments. All of those things can be lost or taken away.

Suppose you suggest that God is the ultimate permanent entity. In that case, I would ask you, 'Who is the one who knows God?' It's crucial to understand that before we can claim that God exists eternally, we must first acknowledge our own existence. The only thing that has remained constant in our lives is the sense that we exist, the feeling of 'I Am'. It's like a spark that's always been inside of us, even before we were capable of thinking or perceiving the world around us. And no matter what happens in our lives, that sense of 'I Am' remains constant. While everything else may be denied, the one thing that cannot be denied is the feeling of 'I Am'. René Descartes was just one step away from this realization when he famously said, 'I think, therefore I am.' One need not engage in thought to experience this state of existence. In fact, this feeling of being, or 'I Am', exists prior to any thought or mental activity.

Consider this: if you were locked in a pitch-black room with no way of seeing your body, and someone asked you if you exist, what would you say? Would you need to see yourself or use your sense faculty to know the answer? No, you would intuitively know it. You don't even need to refer to your mind to say that you are. This sense of existence is ingrained within us and doesn't rely on our thoughts to prove it.

But, you may ask, how can 'I' be permanent? I will die in time. This idea that 'I' will die in time is based on an assumption that death is a natural and inevitable part of existence. However, have you ever experienced your own non-existence? The truth is that death is merely a construct, and just because we observe it happening to others, we assume it will happen to us too. It all depends on how we define ourselves. If we view ourselves solely as physical bodies or as the sum of our thoughts and emotions, then yes, our existence may be limited. But if we recognize that our true Self is Awareness itself, then our existence is eternal and ever-present.

The sense of 'I Am' is the foundation of all experiences, and it's available to us at every moment. While our breaths may pause at times, the feeling of existence, which is expressed as the 'I Am', always remains constant. To have any experience, there must be an experiencer present.

The desired effect of holding on to 'I Am' is to cross over from the known to the unknown, from the verbal to the non-verbal. The sense of 'I Am' can be both real and unreal, depending on how we relate to it. If we identify it with an object or idea, it becomes unreal. However, when we detach it from the knower and the known, the sense of 'I Am' becomes real. It is the space where the experiencer and the experienced arise, dance and dissolve. It is the force that empowers both, yet it remains hidden. Just as electricity powers a light bulb or a fan, but cannot be seen directly, the presence of 'I am' is inferred by its ability to energize. Discovering that we are the Source of our being, beyond our physical appearance, is the ultimate act of self-discovery.

'I Am' serves as a powerful link between the manifested and the unmanifested. 'I Am' is the expression of the love between the inner and the outer. It is our doorway to the realm of the infinite. Just as a dream is tied together by the existence of the dreamer, the waking world can be tied together by the existence of the Awareness that is beyond it. The 'I Am' is the key to unlocking this Awareness. Holding on to 'I Am' can work as a great anchor and help·train our minds. Time and again, we find ourselves caught up in the tribulations of our own personhood. It can be hard to see beyond our own struggles and challenges. But if we shift our attention from the screen of our thoughts to the sense of 'I Am', we can break free from that spell.

The best way to recognize the Awareness is to be the Awareness, and the best medium to be the Awareness is to hold on to the sense of 'I Am'.

The Source of 'I Am'

The Source of 'I Am' is rooted in silence—a state free from movement, noise and impulse. When we immerse ourselves in this state of silence, we transcend the limitations of time and space, and experience profound rest and peace. We bask in the boundless light and bliss of our being.

Once we have tasted this absorption in the Self, we realize that no worldly pleasure can compare to this state of bliss. It feels like returning home to a place of ultimate fulfilment. It's no wonder that meditation is called 'dhyana' in Sanskrit, which means 'remembering'. We already possess this state of being within ourselves; we just need a gentle reminder to reconnect with it.

There is a beautiful story about Hanuman, who is known for his role in the Hindu epic Ramayana, in helping Lord Rama rescue his wife Sita from the demon king Ravana. Hanuman had several boons of immortality, strength and wisdom from God. But, knowing that Hanuman was still a child and could misuse his powers, God decided to make him forget his powers until someone reminded him of them. This was why Jambavan, an immortal and wise person, had to remind Hanuman of his powers. Once Hanuman was reminded of his powers by Jambavan, he went on to use them for great deeds and to help others.

The story of Hanuman can be seen as a metaphor for the human condition and the potential that lies within each individual. Like Hanuman, we all have innate powers such as immortality, wisdom and strength, but we may have forgotten about them or not yet realized them fully. Sita, being held hostage by the demon king Ravana, can represent the way in which our attention is captured and held by the ego self and its desires, leading us away from our true nature. And when Hanuman is reminded of his powers and uses them to help rescue Sita and bring her back to Lord Rama, it symbolizes the process of awakening and returning to our true nature as Awareness. The story serves as a reminder to each of us that the process of Self-realization is to bring attention back to the Awareness, instead of investing it in the egoic self, which rises as compulsive thoughts every moment.

Tuning in to the silence is almost like tuning a radio to the right signal, the frequency at which the emanation from the inner Self is possible. If we can stay tuned to the silence at the Source, we don't need any intermediary practices. All our past mental conditioning are purified by a kind of osmosis.

Diving into the Oceanic Depths of the Here and Now

There is no space for the fluctuations of the mind in the here and now. Anchoring our mind to the present moment means not giving space for the mind to wander into the past or future. It's about being aware and alert in the present. In the present moment, we experience true freedom. The stories that keep us trapped are simply memories, and therefore unreliable. Seeking fulfilment in the past or the future is fruitless. We are already whole and complete in the here and now. The urge to escape the present moment is an indication that we believe that something in the future or past will complete us. True perfection can only be attained when our actions arise from the depth of our being, which is already whole and complete.

What does it mean to stay in the now and what is the now, after all? Anything we point out and say is 'now', has already become the past by the time we point it out. 'Now' is related to time, yet is not limited by it. Instead, it's a kind of doorway to the timeless realm of being. Staying in the now requires a shift in perspective from thinking of the now as a moment in time to experiencing it as a state of being.

Every passing moment becomes a memory, including the scene you saw just moments ago. The present moment is constantly renewing, and even the tree you're looking at is changing and growing older by the second. Although it may seem like you're looking at the same tree, it's actually continuously evolving.

To fully engage with the present, take a moment to notice anything in front of you. There's a clear and undeniable difference between the present moment and memory. While we might think the difference lies in intensity, the truth is that the presence of Awareness makes the present moment feel more real. When we're remembering or anticipating something, we're accessing our minds. But in the present moment, we're primarily aware of our presence and Awareness, which is not a creation of our minds.

This is why the present moment feels more real than the past or future. We carry the sense of the 'here and now' with us wherever we go, a reminder that we're not limited by space and time. In reality, space and time are merely appearances within us. Our strong identification with the body creates an illusion of finiteness, but in truth, we are infinite and eternal beings. The witnessing consciousness can never be accessed anywhere but the here and now.

Unlearning and Embracing a Thought-Free State

Have you ever felt weighed down by all the knowledge and beliefs you've accumulated throughout your life? What if all that information is actually holding you back from experiencing new perspectives and possibilities? Maybe it's time to take off that heavy backpack of knowledge and explore a thought-free state. Imagine being free from the confines of your own mind and experiencing the world around you without judgement or preconceived notions.

It's a radical idea—that all knowledge is a form of bondage. After all, how many times have our beliefs and ideas limited us or prevented us from seeing things in a new light? By unlearning and embracing a thought-free state, we can break free from these limitations and experience true freedom.

Of course, unlearning is not an easy process—we generally cling too tightly to what we think we know. Unlearning requires letting go of our attachments and being open to new possibilities. But the rewards are worth it. When we enter into a thought-free state, we can truly be present in the moment and experience life without the filter of our own biases. It's a liberating and transformational experience that opens up new doors of exploration.

The art of handling any situation lies in the ability to release the thoughts that are associated with it. Just as you can let go of an object by simply releasing it from your hand, you can train your mind to relinquish every thought, no matter how significant it may seem to appear. Remember that the world will continue to function even if you take a brief pause from thinking. To facilitate this, you can conjure up an image of striking off each thought from the surface of the mind with a swift flick, much like the act of hitting a coin during a game of carrom.

The thought-free state is our portal to what lies beyond, to the reality of our Self. By maintaining this state for an extended period, we can experience a profound absorption in our true 'Self'. Something from inside will rise and consume us, leaving nothing behind. This experience of absorption or samadhi is incredibly profound and transformative. It is a gateway to the infinite potential that lies within us. The experience can be life-changing as it gives you a taste of expanse and oneness. With continued practice, the state of absorption becomes more accessible. Experiment with any of these portals with earnestness and you will be liberated.

The Second Mode of Cultivation of Pure Awareness

This mode is one of effortless relaxation, where we let go of all efforts and allow the mind to naturally unfold. Rather than trying to discipline the mind, the focus is on clear seeing and understanding. We cultivate a sense of Awareness characterized by unconditional acceptance and openness, where we invite whatever arises without resistance or attachment. With this understanding, we can fully embrace the activities of our minds. Ashtavakra Gita mentions that the Self is ever-present, and it is the only reality. The wise person sees the Self in all beings, and all beings in the Self.

Releasing Effort and Relaxing Attention

To continue our journey, we need to turn our attention outwards once again. Instead of sinking deeper into our inner selves, we must face the world and engage with objects, activities and relationships. We must strive to embody our new-found understanding in every aspect of our lives, from our daily activities to our most intimate relationships.

Whether we're swimming in the ocean or stargazing at night, the presence of Awareness imbues all experiences equally. By recognizing this, we can enter into a transcendent meditative state in which we knowingly exist as the Awareness amidst the presence of objects.

In this state, objects can no longer distract us from our true nature because all objects are simply a reflection of our own consciousness. So, if we're swimming and we're aware that our experience arises within the field of Awareness, is perceived by the presence of Awareness, and is composed of the Awareness in which it arises, then we're already in a state of transcendental meditation. We don't need to search any further for harmony and inner peace. This is the state of sahaja samadhi, a state that goes beyond even the highest level of *nirvikalpa* samadhi, which is a state of absorption into pure bliss without the use of objects. However, the state of nirvikalpa samadhi eventually comes to an end, whereas sahaja samadhi is a state of being that is continuous. In this mode, meditation is not a distinct activity that starts or stops, but rather the inherent nature of our experience. Whether we are sitting in stillness with our eyes closed or engaging in any other activity, we remain in a state of meditation. We don't label one activity as meditation and another as not, but rather recognize that all activities are equally infused with the presence of Awareness.

We can view this as a release from the addiction of identifying as a wave, constantly striving to reach one shore while avoiding the other. Instead, we surrender to our nature as water, becoming one with the vastness of the ocean and relinquishing our attachment to any specific form, and in embracing the state of being nothing in particular, we realize that we are, in fact, everything.

When we are too focused on Awareness, we want to get rid of the mind and the mind becomes our biggest enemy. We are always seeking a thought-free state but the truth is that the mind and the Awareness can coexist—we don't have to choose one over the other. To understand this mode better, imagine Awareness as a white canvas and our mind with all its thoughts and experiences as a vibrant painting with different colours and forms. Consider the following three situations:

In the first, we are absorbed and lost in the painting completely. Overtaken by the forms and colours used, we forget the white canvas underneath. This is how we are when we are completely consumed by our thoughts and experiences and forget the background of Awareness.

In the second, we step back from the painting and focus on the white canvas itself. This is almost like stepping back from the chaos of the mind with its thoughts and experiences and focusing on Awareness itself.

In the third, we are aware of the painting while still maintaining Awareness of the white canvas. We see both the canvas and the paint at the same time. This allows us to fully appreciate the beauty of the art. This is like observing the activities of the mind while being fully aware of the fact that it appears in Awareness, allowing us to appreciate the beauty of life with all its experiences.

At a certain point, it's possible for the line between consciousness, and the things it perceives, to blur and eventually disappear, leading to a state where there is no differentiation between the Self and the unfolding of experience itself. This collapse of boundaries opens up a new way of experiencing the world, where the barriers between subject and object dissolve into a seamless whole.

5

Results: Rebirth as a Spiritual Being

'We are not human beings having a spiritual experience. We are spiritual beings having a human experience.'—Teilhard de Chardin

The key to alleviating our deepest struggles lies in the discovery of our true essence as Awareness, the very fabric of existence, consciousness and bliss. This profound realization transcends mere temporary solutions and ushers us into a lasting state of inner peace and fulfilment. Our true liberation does not come from transforming the individual 'person' we believe ourselves to be, but rather from relinquishing the very concept of 'personhood' altogether. Every challenge becomes an opportunity to identify the impurities in the mind and alchemize them by offering them into the light of Awareness.

Our world is limited and repetitive as long as we are ignorant of our real Self as the creator. Once we go beyond our self-imposed limitations, we unlock the power to manifest the world of our dreams, where harmony and beauty thrive. When we continue to abide in pure Awareness and transcend our limited sense of self, we become more godlike, embodying the qualities of the divine that manifest within and through us. Life takes on a mystical and magical quality.

An Awakened Mind and An Awakened World

An awakened mind is a powerful creator as it recognizes itself as the pure Awareness that is the Source of all beings. As pure Awareness, we are already complete, and it is through this fullness that the world rises within us. The world is a product of our inherent joy. The creation of this world is not an error, but a play. The good news is we are ever free and untouched by this play of duality.

As soon as we step back from our identified minds, we become expansive and understand all things. We enter a space where we can embrace the all, yet be attached to none. An awakened mind has the ability to quiet its own thoughts and can rest in a state of stillness for any length of time; while engaged in action, it has the capability of perfecting all actions.

We must eliminate any doubts and trust that everything is happening for our ultimate good. The intelligence behind the design of the universe is perfect, and therefore, we can have complete confidence in it. This design can never go wrong, so we should release all our insecurities and surrender to the perfection of the universe.

The knowledge that we are the Awareness transforms us into powerful creators of an awakened world. It is akin to the lucid dream state, where we realize that we are dreaming and can consciously participate in and shape our dream. With this Awareness, we can transform even the darkest nightmare into the most beautiful dream.

According to the ancient yogic text, Patanjali Yoga Sutras, the practice of yoga (union with the highest self) leads to the attainment of supernatural abilities or *Vibhutis*. These powers are not an end in themselves but are seen as stepping stones on the path to spiritual realization. As we awaken to our true nature as pure Awareness, we begin to access the supernatural powers inherent within us. These powers include clairvoyance, telepathy and even the ability to shape reality itself. However, it is essential to use these powers with utmost discretion and only for the highest good. Ultimately, the attainment of these supernatural abilities is not the goal of yoga but rather a natural by-product of spiritual practice. As we continue to deepen our understanding of the true Self and the nature of reality, we become vessels for divine consciousness to flow through us. We become instruments of the divine, using our abilities to serve the world and uplift humanity.

Living to Benefit All

The question of how to lead our lives has puzzled us all for centuries. On the one hand, the experience of samadhi and the realization that all is an illusion may lead one to believe that the only path forward is to completely isolate oneself and focus solely on spiritual practice to stay absorbed. However, on the other hand, the world we live in is very real to us and requires us to engage with it in some way. So, how do we bridge the gap between knowing and doing?

One approach is to embrace the tool of compassion and loving-kindness in our interactions with the world. By understanding that the world is a projection of the Self, we can use our actions to create positive ripples in the world. We can engage with the world in a way that is beneficial to ourselves and others, without becoming attached to the outcomes.

At the same time, it is important to cultivate a mindset of detachment, like a monk. This doesn't mean that we should completely detach ourselves from the world, but rather we should approach our interactions with a sense of non-attachment. We must learn to observe our thoughts and emotions without becoming entangled in them.

From time to time, we can adopt exercises such as going for retreats and completely disconnecting from the world, and engaging in deeper practice. This can help us recharge and when we come back to our daily lives, we can bring the benefits of our practice with us. It's important to remember that the ultimate goal is not just personal enlightenment or liberation, but also the alleviation of the suffering of all beings.

In the Tao Te Ching, it is proclaimed—'Therefore the Master takes action by letting things take their course. He remains as calm at the end as at the beginning. He has nothing and thus has nothing to lose. What he desires is non-desire; what he learns is to unlearn. He simply reminds people of who they have always been. He cares about nothing but the Tao. Thus he can care for all things.'

Overflowing Love and Compassion for All

Incessant thinking is a symptom of a diseased mind that is in a constant state of lack. Driven by greed and fear, it is always calculating how it can benefit from any situation or person—a constant engagement that keeps it in a perpetual state of unease. But through the power of knowledge when we shed our 'ego', the mind shifts from a 'what's-in-it-for-me' mentality to a 'how-can-I-contribute' mindset.

As we release our ego, we become a source of strength for others rather than a burden, a transformation that embodies the essence of unconditional love. Love is an energy that gives; it is an intense experience in one's inner space. It is not something that we can force or create through effort. Love is what happens to us when we are connected to our real 'self'. In a state of connectedness, we experience overflowing love towards all. It's like a stream of love that flows out to wherever it's needed, without any effort or doership on our part. This is the ultimate experience of being human, to embody and share the boundless love that is our true nature.

Love is Deeply Healing

Love is a powerful force that can heal even the deepest of wounds and traumas. It can transform our lives and those of the people around us. It has the ability to mend broken hearts, alleviate pain, and bring a sense of wholeness and restoration to our lives. However, not all forms of love are equal. Love can manifest itself in many different ways, ranging from selfish and possessive to selfless and pure.

Selfish love is often characterized by possessiveness, insecurity and jealousy. It can be harmful and toxic, causing pain and suffering for both the giver and the receiver. This type of love is often focused on satisfying one's own desires and needs, rather than considering the well-being of the other person. On the other hand, selfless love is infused with purity and spirituality and always pushes us to transcend the boundaries of our own ego. It is characterized by a deep sense of compassion and empathy, where one is willing to put the needs of others above one's own. This type of love is focused on giving and nurturing, rather than taking and controlling.

Research has shown that love has a significant impact on our physical, emotional and mental well-being, and it can help us live longer, happier and healthier lives. In a research study conducted by the Harvard Study of Adult Development, it was found that people who were in strong, loving relationships were happier and healthier than those who were not. The study followed participants for over seventy-five years, and found that those who were in supportive relationships were more likely to live longer, experience less stress and have better overall health. In addition, a study by the American Psychological Association found that couples who show affection and support for each other are more likely to have lower levels of the stress hormone—Cortisol.* High levels of cortisol have been linked to a range of health problems, including cardiovascular disease, weakened immune systems and obesity.

---

* Vaillant, G. E. (2012). Triumphs of Experience: The Men of the Harvard Grant Study. Cambridge, MA: Belknap Press.

Another study conducted by the Harvard Medical School shows that people who have strong and supportive relationships tend to have lower rates of depression, anxiety and stress-related illnesses and are more likely to recover from major illnesses or surgeries.* Furthermore, studies have shown that love and positive social interactions can even affect our genetic make-up, leading to better physical health and a longer lifespan.† In short, the healing power of love is not just a poetic metaphor—it is a scientifically proven fact.

The Transformative Power of Loving Kindness and Compassion

One of the main characteristics that set living beings apart from non-living beings is the experience of pain. Even the most advanced machine or AI cannot feel the pain that an ant can experience. All living beings, from the smallest creatures to humans, share a common desire for happiness and a wish to avoid pain or suffering. This fundamental truth bolsters the need to cultivate a good heart and loving compassion as the most important aspect of our lives.

The golden rule of treating others as we would like to be treated is based on this fundamental truth. As we cultivate mindfulness, we deepen our ability to empathize with

---

* Kiecolt-Glaser, J. K., and Newton, T. L. (2001). Marriage and health: his and hers. *Psychological Bulletin*, 127(4), 472–503.
† Cole, S. W., Hawkley, L. C., Arevalo, J. M. G., and Cacioppo, J. T. (2011). Transcript origin analysis identifies antigen-presenting cells as primary targets of socially regulated gene expression in leukocytes. *Proceedings of the National Academy of Sciences*, 108(7), 3080–85.

others and see things from their perspective. This allows us to begin to understand the roots of dysfunctionality and the circumstances that lead individuals to behave in hurtful ways.

Nobody is born cruel—a newborn baby radiates pure love and innocence. It's the circumstances of life that shape us and lead us down different paths. By examining the conditions that have shaped an individual's life, we can begin to see why they behave in certain ways and what factors contribute to their actions. This understanding leads us to a place of forgiveness and compassion. When we see others in this light, it becomes easier to extend kindness, generosity and respect to all beings, even those who have caused us harm.

Throughout our lives, we will encounter people who treat us poorly or attempt to make us feel worthless, often due to their own negative experiences. However, by looking through a lens of compassion, we can begin to understand their story and the circumstances that led them to behave in such a way. Perhaps they were subjected to bad parenting or unfavourable circumstances that cause them to repeat the unconscious patterns that they were subjected to. Likewise, we may come across individuals with abrasive personalities who are quick to criticize and slow to forgive. Yet, with the practice of mindfulness and compassion, we can shift our perspective and delve deeper into their actions to understand the root causes. As we explore their story, we may discover the pain and suffering that lies beneath their tough exteriors, such as growing up in poverty, experiencing hunger, illness or constant fear. As a result, they may have become self-reliant and guarded, pushing others away to protect themselves from further pain.

Through our practice of loving kindness and compassion, we can see anybody's story with new eyes. We can see the pain and suffering that lie underneath everyone's behaviour and can respond with empathy and understanding. And in doing so, we are able to offer them the love and support they need to heal and transform their lives. Compassionate Awareness heals and redeems.

No matter how wealthy we are, if we lack compassion, there is no peace and satisfaction in our lives. Even if we came to own everything on earth, we would still be dissatisfied. Without developing our minds and practising compassion, there is no way to find peace and satisfaction in our lives. No matter how much fame, power or education we have, if loving compassion is missing from our lives, we will never be truly happy.

The Neuroscience of Loving Kindness and Compassion

Practising love and compassion has a profound effect on the way our brain processes emotions and experiences. When we engage in acts of love and compassion, it activates the reward centre of our brain, releasing hormones like dopamine and oxytocin which are associated with pleasure, bonding and social connection. This leads to a positive mindset and the ability to regulate negative emotions, resulting in greater emotional resilience and a sense of well-being.

Studies have shown that individuals who regularly engage in loving kindness meditation have increased grey matter density in brain regions associated with emotional regulation, empathy and perspective-taking.* This indicates that practising love and compassion can change the structure and function of our brains, promoting positive mental health.

Beautiful Flowering Relationships

Without compassion, it's easy to fall into a pattern of seeing others as potential enemies, rather than friends. When we lack empathy and understanding, we may interpret others' actions in a negative light and respond with hostility or defensiveness.

For example, imagine we have a disagreement with a friend over a minor issue. Without compassion, we might quickly jump to the conclusion that our friend is being deliberately difficult or trying to undermine us. This could lead to an argument or a breakdown in our relationship, all because we didn't take the time to understand our friend's perspective and show them kindness and respect.

On the other hand, if we approach the situation with compassion, we might take a step back and try to see things from our friend's point of view. We might realize that they have a valid reason for their behaviour, or that they're dealing with their own personal struggles. By extending empathy and understanding, we can avoid turning our friend into an enemy and instead, work towards a resolution that benefits everyone involved.

---

* Hölzel, B. K., Carmody, J., Vangel, M., Congleton, C., Yerramsetti, S. M., Gard, T., and Lazar, S. W. (2011). Mindfulness practice leads to increases in regional brain gray matter density. *Psychiatry Research: Neuroimaging*, 191(1), 36–43.

When we cultivate compassion, we're able to approach others with kindness and understanding, which can help us build better and more harmonious relationships. We start to see others as fellow human beings with their own struggles and aspirations, rather than as potential enemies or obstacles in our lives. Compassion also helps us to communicate more effectively and resolve conflicts more peacefully. When we approach a situation with empathy and understanding, we're more likely to listen to other's perspectives and find common ground. This can lead to more productive and positive outcomes, rather than escalating tension and conflict. And when we extend compassion to others, we often find that they respond in kind. When we treat others with kindness and respect, they're more likely to do the same for us, creating a cycle of positive energy that can ripple outwards to others.

Being compassionate can help us have more enlightened and fulfilling relationships, whether it's with our friends, partners, children or parents. When we cultivate compassion, we become more attuned to the needs and feelings of others, and we're able to respond to them in a way that's supportive and nurturing. This can help us build deeper connections with people and create a sense of trust and mutual respect that can sustain us through difficult times. Here are a few examples of how compassion can lead to more enlightened relationships.

With our children: Imagine your child is having a tantrum because they're feeling overwhelmed and frustrated. Without compassion, you might respond with frustration or anger, adding fuel to the fire. But with compassion, you might take a step back and try to understand what's driving your child's behaviour. You might recognize that they're feeling tired or hungry, or that they're struggling with a particular challenge. By responding with empathy and support, you can help your child feel heard and validated, and create a stronger bond between the two of you.

With our partners: Imagine your partner has made a mistake that's caused a rift in your relationship. Without compassion, you might respond with blame or anger, pushing your partner away and creating more distance between you. But with compassion, you might approach the situation with empathy and understanding. You might recognize that your partner is human, and prone to making mistakes, just like you are. By responding with kindness and forgiveness, you can create a sense of mutual trust and respect that can help your relationship grow stronger over time.

With our friends: Imagine your friend is going through a tough time and is feeling down and discouraged. Without compassion, you might respond with dismissiveness or judgement, making your friend feel even worse. But with compassion, you might take the time to listen to your friend's concerns, and offer support and encouragement. You might recognize that your friend is dealing with their own struggles and that your kindness and understanding can make a real difference in their life. By responding with compassion, you can strengthen your friendship and create a more supportive, nurturing relationship.

In all of these examples, compassion allows us to approach relationships with empathy and understanding, rather than judgement or blame. It is essential for building and maintaining healthy relationships with others, whether they're friends, family members or acquaintances. By recognizing the humanity in others, and responding with kindness and support, we can create relationships that are more enlightened, fulfilling and supportive for everyone involved.

Ending the Cycle of Pain through Compassion

'*What is broken can be mended. What hurts can be healed. And no matter how dark it gets, the sun is going to rise again.*'— Ernest Hemingway

The cycle of pain and suffering can be a difficult pattern to break. It can be deeply ingrained in our familial and societal patterns and may go unnoticed for generations, perpetuating a cycle of negativity and struggle. It is up to us to recognize this pattern and take responsibility for breaking the cycle. We can end the cycle by transmuting our own pain and the pain of others by grounding it into our Awareness, much like a lightning rod takes lightning and grounds it into the earth. When we experience pain that triggers us, we can view it as a call to action. It is asking us to break the cycle of suffering and create a new path forward for ourselves.

To do so, we must first become self-aware and practise mindfulness. By paying attention to our thoughts, feelings and behaviours, we can begin to recognize the patterns that keep us trapped in cycles of negativity. This process can be difficult, as it may require us to confront painful experiences and emotions. We must hold our traumas and dysfunctional patterns in the loving embrace of Awareness.

The transmutation of our own suffering enables us to transmute the suffering of people around us as we extend our compassion to them. Through this practice, we can create a ripple effect of healing and renewal, spreading it and breaking the cycle of pain and suffering that may have been present in our families and the world at large for generations.

By ending the cycle of pain, we can create a brighter future for ourselves and those around us. We can become agents of change in our communities, spreading love, peace and understanding. It is up to every one of us to take responsibility for our own healing and to choose to break the cycle of pain and suffering, creating a new pattern of hope and positivity.

It is all part of a Cosmic Art,
The universe itself is a masterpiece of the Divine heart.

Though we may seem separate, with differences apparent,
In oneness, we find freedom, a truth so inherent.
For when we see the differences, but feel no separation,
We are truly free, in a world of infinite creation.

Oneness is in play if we only choose to see,
From the dance of the stars to the bustle of the bees.
It's in the laughter of the child, and the tears of the old,
Where the magic of oneness begins to unfold.

Oneness is in the power of our dreams, and the faith that we hold,
In the strength of our spirit, and the fire in our soul.
It's in the touch of a loved one, and the kindness of a stranger,
In the power of forgiveness, and the grace of surrender.

For oneness is in play, if we only choose to see,
A Divine force, that forever will be.

Through the thread of 'I am', we're guided home,
To the heart of oneness, the transcendental Source.
Where kindness and compassion reign supreme,
And perfection in action is no longer a dream.

Acknowledgements

The creation of *Pain: A Portal to Enlightenment* has been made possible through the generous contributions of several remarkable individuals. Their unwavering support and expertise have played a crucial role in shaping this book, and I am deeply grateful for their involvement in this endeavour.

First and foremost, I would like to extend my heartfelt gratitude to Vishal Kirti. Vishal's patient collaboration and unwavering commitment to refining the content of this book were instrumental in shaping it into the concrete and meaningful work it has become. His dedication to this project has been a wellspring of inspiration and I consider myself fortunate to have had him as a cornerstone throughout this endeavour.

I am deeply indebted to Nitin Pabuwal for his exceptional work during the editing process. Nitin's keen insights, meticulous attention to detail and valuable suggestions have significantly enhanced the quality of this book. His expertise has been invaluable, and I'm grateful for his involvement.

In times when writer's block threatened to impede progress, I found solace in the guidance of Swami Sarvapriyananda. His wisdom and support were instrumental in overcoming the creative challenges that emerged along the way. Swami Sarvapriyananda's insights were like a beacon of light, guiding me forward, and I'm thankful for his presence.

A special acknowledgement goes to Milee Ashwarya, Dipanjali Chadha and Saba Nehal, who generously lent their editing skills to refine this work. Their dedication and commitment to excellence have been truly commendable, and their contributions have undoubtedly made a significant impact on the final outcome of the book.

In closing, I want to express my deep appreciation to all those who played a role, whether big or small, in bringing *Pain: A Portal to Enlightenment* to fruition. Your collective contributions have woven a tapestry of knowledge and insight, and I am humbled by the collaborative effort that has made this work possible. Thank you for being part of this journey.

Scan QR code to access the
Penguin Random House India website